SOLD OUT

Taking the lid off evangelism

Clive Calver

Lakeland

MARSHALL, MORGAN & SCOTT

Lakeland
Marshall, Morgan & Scott
a Pentos company
1 Bath Street, London EC1V 9LB

First published by Marshall, Morgan & Scott 1980

Unless otherwise stated biblical quotations are from the
Revised Standard Version of the Bible, copyrighted 1946
and 1952, © 1971 and 1973 by the Division of Christian
Education of the National Council of the Churches of
Christ in the USA. Biblical quotations identified NEB
are from the New English Bible, TEV from Today's English
Version, LB from the Living Bible, NASB from the New
American Standard Bible.

The title of chapter one is taken from the Malcolm and
Alwyn song of the same title.
The following poems and songs are used by permission:
pp. 19-20 'Paradise Now' by Julien Beck.
pp. 34-5 'All' by Michel Quoist from *Prayers of Life*,
published by Gill and Son, 1963.
p. 53 'Battle Hymn' by Graham Kendrick from the LP
The Fighter, recorded by Kingsway.
p. 76 *The old college try* by Wes Seeliger, published by
Forum House, Atlanta, USA.
pp. 98-9 'Let us open up ourselves' by Dave Bilborough
from the LP *Dave Bilborough and Friends*, recorded by
Kingsway.

ISBN: 0 551 00827 X

Printed in Great Britain by
Hunt Barnard Printing Ltd., Aylesbury, Bucks.
9711M01

Acknowledgments

We are slowly learning, within the Church of Christ, that we owe so much to so many of our brothers and sisters. My very deep thanks go to everyone who has been involved in the publication of *Sold Out*. I do want to give a special thank you to those who involved themselves so willingly in order that this book could be produced.

I am grateful to my secretary Gail Gwilt and also to Sharon Green, Pauline Moreton, Marion Rowlands and Marjorie Frith for helping to type the manuscript. To Gilbert Kirby for the Foreword, Phil Thomson for the cover and art work and Mike Morris for all those patient rewrites. My gratitude goes to all the staff at Marshalls and especially Rachel Maurice, my editor, for never failing to give maximum support. I am thankful to Charles Henshall of Kingsway Publications for getting me going, to Pete Meadows of Buzz for all his advice and encouragement, and to Rob Buckeridge who helped to write much of the background material for chapters six and seven.

Youth for Christ gave me the time and my wife and family had to live with me while the book was being written; they know how thrilled I am to have such support. Finally I will always be grateful to Roger Forster, George Tarleton and Philip Vogel because years ago they first taught me by their lives and words, to begin to understand what it really means to be 'Sold Out'.

Contents

Foreword

Not everyone – particularly among those of my generation! – is going to like this book. It is too radical, too honest. It is a little too near the bone for those of us brought up in the age of easy-believism. Some of us have been fortunate enough to have been thrown in the deep end by being brought into close contact with the rising generation of young evangelicals. They are very different from the old brigade. Frankly, they seem to take their Christian commitment rather more seriously. They say some shocking things. They repudiate respectable middle-class Christianity in favour of radical discipleship. They try to take our Lord's words at their face value – something which some of us of vintage years have hesitated to do.

I count it a privilege to write a foreword to this book even though some of my contemporaries may wonder how I could possibly do so. I happen to belong to that group of older Christians which does not write off the younger generation as irreverent and irresponsible. Fourteen years as Principal of the London Bible College has taught me much more than I have been able to teach. Outwardly, some of the young people with whom I have worked might not appear to be 'dedicated'. They do not fit into the neat evangelical mould shaped by the tradition of the elders. They ask embarrassing questions. They want to know why we do not do certain things and why we do some other things. They find that often it is difficult, if not impossible, to see any real relationship between life in the local church and life in the New Testament Church. Some of us are learning slowly and at times reluctantly from these young men and women. We find them a bit outspoken at times but we are getting the message.

I suppose I ought to 'come clean'. The author of this book is no casual acquaintance. He studied at the College of which I was Principal and subsequently married the Principal's daughter! After some years heading up an evangelical team, he accepted the invitation to become National Director of British Youth for Christ of which I have the honour to be President.

Clive Calver, under God, has been used to give a face-lift to that movement so that today it is one of the most dynamic Christian youth movements in the country. He has also associated himself with various activities associated with the Evangelical Alliance. I have rarely met a young man with such boundless energy. He is essentially an 'ideas' man. He is always one move ahead but he has a way of persuading his Board to back him. This book will give its readers a pretty good idea of the sort of man Clive is. Some will write him off as just another of those 'angry young men' who never seem to grow up. Perhaps it is as well for the Church of God that some of them don't! In a sense there is nothing new here, it only sounds that way because we haven't heard this note struck too often in our time. We are simply being asked to take Christ seriously, to reassess our methods of presenting the gospel and rediscover authentic evangelism as exemplified in the New Testament. I would like to see this book read and acted upon. Only truly dedicated disciples can meet the challenge of our secular society. It is a sad commentary on our time that we have to speak of 'committed Christians' – can there truly be any other variety?

The 1980s have been set aside as 'a decade for evangelism'. It is our earnest hope and prayer that we shall see such evangelism conducted on truly biblical lines, that the invitation will not be simply to 'accept Christ as Saviour', but 'to repent and believe the gospel' with all that implies. It was such evangelism which transformed British society following the preaching of the Wesleys and of George Whitfield. 'Only believism' will not lead to that radical change of life-style which is the most urgent need of our time. To repent implies a total reorientation of life, a right about turn. May God raise up an increasing number of evangelists who will not flinch from declaiming 'the whole counsel of God'.!

Gilbert W. Kirby

Prologue

God . . .
        What have you done?
        What have we done?
I just don't understand . . .
How could you, a loving heavenly Father
The God of history
Sovereign Lord of the cosmos
How could you make such a dreadful mistake?
Why did it all fall apart,
                so very
                very
                quickly
Lord, ignoring the possibilities of some accidental
malfunction in the divine computer.
Or the ridiculous suggestion that your cosmic
design broke down.
Or that Satan for just one round out-pointed the
Holy One of Israel. Lord,
Knowing your Spirit will never be thwarted,
Please can you explain?

Why did our love die?
Why did we turn away?'
Why, if you didn't do it, did you let us?
What have we done Lord

To your church
   your world
   your nation?
Why Lord?
Where will it all end?

1:

, . . . England Goodbye'

Sunday evening. Six thirty p.m. It's the 'Gospel' service again. You sit quietly and squirm inside at the 'message'. Nothing too complicated, a very simple message but with that recognisable flavour of familiarity which makes you say to yourself, 'I've heard it all before.'

Oh no! Now he's going to make an appeal. They don't usually go that far. It's obviously a well-practised, yet colourful appeal; 'Jesus is calling tonight. Will you accept him as *your* Saviour and friend? He is patiently waiting at the door of your heart; why not open that door and let him in. You know that *now* could be your time. How long will you reject his offer of love, joy, peace, satisfaction and happiness? All you need to do is believe in Jesus. Ask him into your heart as we sing this closing hymn; ask and he'll come right now.'

Up and down this land that 'Gospel' is proclaimed Sunday by Sunday in hundreds of pulpits. Faithful men repeating what they have been taught, unwittingly misleading people by a simple confidence trick; an invitation to receive an imaginary salvation. In Sunday schools, Bible classes, youth clubs, and personal conversations the pattern is repeated; honest, sincere people – but failing to understand what the gospel really is!

3

So how has this tragic misunderstanding occurred? Is it the result of our tremendous 'numbers-consciousness'; the way we love to calculate and record the number of 'decisions' made in any meeting or campaign? Could it be that our love of tradition has programmed us blindly to accept and repeat parrot-fashion the trite formulae of our spiritual forefathers? Or is it that, paralysed with our desire for results, we have followed the standards of secular society and tried to market the gospel in a way which will be acceptable to it? Whatever the reason may be its conclusion is positively frightening. We have uncomprehendingly sacrificed depth in our message for breadth in statistics and prostituted the very gospel of Jesus by selling it to the lowest bidder!

This might all be justified, to some minds, had the strategy proved successful. In fact, it has been an utter failure. This wishy-washy, watered down pseudo-gospel of the twentieth century has totally repelled the very people whom we surmised it should have attracted. Our contemporary society has not even graced such a gospel with opposition, all that such a message has evoked can be classified as a total, blank indifference! The forces of secularism contentedly go their way knowing that in the absence of the true proclamation of Jesus they have nothing to fear.

In Britain we live with the memory of a nominal Christianity and the respectability of church attendance. Today, while 98 per cent of the population are buried with the words 'in sure and certain hope of the resurrection' pronounced over them, less than 3 per cent remain active churchgoers. When compared with 40 per cent of the population in the United States and 25 per cent in Canada who still regularly attend church, one can see the dreadful decline in even nominal Christianity which has gone on for sixty years. In the light of third world situations which some of us still naïvely regard as 'our mission fields', the contrast is even more stark. In 1900 $7\frac{1}{2}$ per cent of Africans were Christian, today that figure is over 33 per cent, while

4

in parts of Latin America the church is growing at three times the birth-rate!

Recent surveys conducted in English schools have shown alarming, if not surprising results: ignorance of the existence of John's gospel; ignorance of who or what Gideon was (let alone which Testament he appears in); and one class of twelve-year-old girls, when asked what a Christian was answered, in all seriousness, 'Please Sir, a Christian is someone who grows their own vegetables.'

While less than 10 per cent of English school children display any real understanding of basic Christianity, some 80 per cent of inner-city senior school children possess a working knowledge of active occult practice, e.g. ouija, levitation, horoscopes, seances, astral projection, or ritual magic. A teacher I know was despairing of finding any means of interesting, let alone teaching, a particularly difficult class of third formers. I suggested that however 'remedial' some of his class might be there was one subject they would know more about than she did, and which was suitable for a school lesson. Later she told me that they had indeed known far more about the Devil and his ways than she did. Perhaps that is why our society has introduced the study of witchcraft as a suitable 'O' level examination subject.

There must be many reasons for the decline in the moral and spiritual standards of a nation. Lack of spirituality in the church coupled with the increasing permissiveness of an unstable society make up a convincing case for the tragic situation of spiritual inertia which exists in Britain today.

To lose something can be carelessness; to lose yourself would be foolishness; to have lost God must be the most unspeakable tragedy of all time. One thing is certain, at a time when men and women worldwide are searching for God and coming into a living encounter with his son, Britain represents a deeper sense of disillusionment with Christianity than is met elsewhere.

When it all began no one can tell: but at the very time when the church and her message needed to be most relevant and biting it was instead seen as a grotesque anachronism meaning little to anybody, with a message which no longer seemed to count. The words of Jesus which brought good news to the poor, release to the captives, recovery of sight to the blind, liberty to those who were oppressed, have been reduced to the level of a smug evangelicalism. Instead of working to promote a dynamic renewal within society the church quite often worked only to preserve the status quo. While other creeds brought hope for the future, Christianity offered only respectability to the present. 'In some regions of the world Christianity has become synonymous with a gay, unconcerned and irrelevant selfishness and communism synonymous with a committed, disciplined, sacrificial way of living.'[1]

In 1954 a missionary in Vietnam was told by a Viet Cong guerrilla officer, 'I would gladly die if I could advance the cause of communism one more mile . . . You know, as you have read to me from the Bible I have come to believe that you Christians have a greater message than that of communism. But I believe that we are going to win the world, for Christianity means something to you, but communism means everything to us.' It is just that kind of passionate, disciplined, sacrificial commitment which Jesus preached we should have, but many are aware that it is just this which we have lost.

The processes which began in the aftermath of the eighteenth-century evangelical awakening accelerated towards their inevitable conclusion – God was laid aside and forgotten, while man looked to himself as the source of all knowledge, the only true reality in life.

What was the result? A living death whose cancer infected the whole of British society. The disease which for so long had been held in check broke out in this century with a vengeance throughout the twenties, thirties and forties, transforming the retreat of the army of God into a

6

rout. Churches emptied, educationalists apostasised. Young people rebelled with a unique intensity. Through the fifties and sixties Christianity lost much of its remaining intellectual credibility, and a population no longer even nominally Christian turned the faith of a nation to a militant atheism, indifferent agnosticism – or both! Only a remnant survived.

Into this graveyard of shattered ideals blew that wind of confusion and restlessness which marked out the 1970s. No longer could people see clear destinations and objectives; the result both locally and nationally became an aimless wandering. In the turmoil of financial insecurity, industrial unrest, the problems of law and order and an uncertain future only two answers have emerged. One has been that old philosophy – let's live for today, tomorrow we die. The other has come from the punk generation which has given a clear demonstration of how it regards the world of the eighties.

Our self-centred, sin-sick, materialistic society knows its sickness but has forgotten the cure. Everything is in a state of flux. Nothing is static. We have tried to exchange the love of God in the hearts of men for a love for man as the supreme deity. The result; emptiness and a deep sense of cosmic loneliness which still afflicts mankind. Paul Tournier summarises it, 'What is the meaning of this nostalgia for perfection which some admit and others hide, but which is inevitably there in every man and woman! It is our homesickness for Paradise . . . the whole of humanity suffers from what we might call the "Paradise Lost" complex. To a world which was made as the garden for men to walk and talk with their creator God came rebellion, rejection and expulsion – since then mankind has groped through the shadow of homesickness searching for a home.'[2]

The situation is further aggravated by a world which refuses to stand still for a moment, even to catch its breath. This is reflected in the way that half the population of the United States move house every year. On our own doorstep marriages are broken as quickly and easily as they are made.

And so a lonely, confused, erratic, spontaneous, lost and troubled world has shouted out for standards, for answers to the questions they really are asking. But the church has stood in stony silence. It was all happening too quickly. Only the sects seized the opportunity to lead men further into falseness, while the light stayed shadowed by its own indifference, and men went on walking in darkness.

It will be to our eternal regret that by tragic neglect we have failed to reach our lost generation with the only genuine alternative to our present society. An alternative summed up in the words of a twentieth-century spokesman who discovered what so many have missed:—

So I came back to where I began, to that other King one Jesus; to the Christian notion that man's efforts to make himself personally and collectively happy in earthly terms are doomed to failure. He must indeed, as Christ said, be born again, be as a new man or he's nothing. So at least I have concluded, having failed to find in the past experience, present dilemmas and future expectations, any alternative proposition. As far as I am concerned, it is Christ or nothing.[3]

Instead of learning how to communicate *to* our day and generation we have learned how to communicate *from* it. We have learned to imitate the advertising techniques of our modern-day society and call it evangelism. And so far from the church turning the world upside down, the opposite has occurred.

Now you begin to see what I mean. It is so easy for the evangelist to descend to the level of being no more than a door-to-door salesman of ready-packaged, bargain offer religion. Such a person seeks, by slick selling techniques, to convince any number of folk to receive this 'new birth',

8

yet is left wondering why so many customers never take the time to investigate their 'free gift' further. Where he had expected to see healthy babies, he is confronted with the tragedy of innumerable stillbirths.

I speak from experience. Some years ago a friend and I were conducting a mission at which over a hundred young people made decisions for Christ. A year passed and I returned to the church to preach on the anniversary of the mission. To my horror only a handful of those who had been 'converted' remained. It would have been easy to blame the church for ineffective follow-up but the truth was far more obvious.

Jesus came preaching 'the gospel of the *kingdom*' and we need to grasp the spiritual realities which must be involved in a transfer from the kingdom of darkness to the kingdom of light. Our eagerness has made us run riot with that which is holy and which requires not our innovation but our obedience.

Some years ago I was invited by a fellow evangelist to address a meeting during a crusade he was conducting. As I spoke, I was encouraged by the Lord assuring me that three or four people in the hall were being challenged by his Spirit. I finished my twenty-minute message with a brief challenge to any who had known the hand of God touching their lives, or were just interested in what had been said, to come and talk further afterwards. The evangelist then proceeded to announce the last hymn – 'Just as I am' – and took the opportunity to enforce the challenge with a seventeen-minute appeal! Now appeals are by no means wrong in themselves, but they are open to the twin abuse of over-intensity and over-emotionalism. Twenty people responded to that appeal – God had promised three or four. I do hope they survived the crush in the counselling room and met the Lord who had been seeking them. Furthermore, I trust that the evangelist and I have been forgiven for ordering God's work for him!

We must realise that Jesus said, 'Go and make disciples'

not 'Go and make converts'. How many spiritual babies were stillborn because we tried to bring the gospel down to our level? Why do we try to make the gospel acceptable, instead of laying the message out in the uncompromising terms that Jesus always used? Today we live in an age when we need to choose. If we are involved in Sunday school teaching, youth groups, open-air work, or just chatting to our friends, do we preach the gospel of much modern-day evangelicalism or the message Jesus constantly reiterated: 'Let a man deny himself, take up his cross and follow me' (Matt. 16:24)? That alone was the message Jesus gave: 'Whoever does not bear his own cross and come after me, cannot be my disciple' (Luke 14:27). But when did we last hear that as a straightforward gospel message? Yes, we often hear it preached to Christians but rarely to the unsaved. If as a message it was good enough for Jesus, we have no right to dilute it. Some things are company policy and remain strictly non-negotiable.

To my mind there are three modern-day concepts which have caused the bulk of the problem. These are:—

1. The idea of Jesus as Saviour only
2. The concept of 'accepting' Jesus
3. The content and meaning of 'belief'

Like most controversial statements they contain an element of truth but have been so over-emphasised as to be distorted beyond their original brief.

1. *Jesus Christ, Saviour,* was one of the earliest creda of the church. An early Christian code message revealed God as the Father, Beginning and End.

```
            A
            P
            A
            T
            E
            R
A  PATERNOSTER  O
            O
            S
            T
            E
            R
            O
```

In the same way the sign of the fish was a coded identification symbol, much like a cross or a Crusader or Covenantor badge. The fish in Greek was ICHTHUS, and the unscrambled code reads like this:

I =	= IESOUS	= JESUS
CH =	= CHRISTOS	= CHRIST
TH =	= THEOS	= GOD
U =	= HUIOS	= SON OF
S =	= SOTER	= SAVIOUR

Jesus Christ, son of God, Saviour. From the very beginning of the church the Saviourhood of Jesus was a major emphasis.

In the Scriptures Jesus is revealed as the King of Kings, Lord of Lords, Son of God, Word of God, and Saviour of the world. I often talk of him as 'Jesus'. Recently I received a letter of rebuke from an elderly Christian who insisted that the total biblical name was 'The Lord Jesus Christ'. Certainly, in the New Testament, Christ's Saviourhood (i.e. his role in bringing us forgiveness, redemption

11

and reconciliation with God) is always joined to his Lordship – he *is* Saviour and Lord.

However, the tendency today has been to over-emphasise Christ's Saviourhood at the expense of his Lordship. How like the world we are! We like the good and easy parts but try to ignore the painful and the sacrificial. To preach Jesus Christ as Saviour without equally emphasising his Lordship may be popular but it is totally unbiblical. And when we do pay lip-service to the word 'Lord' it passes without further explanation.

The reaction against this easy-believist gospel is spreading. The Lausanne Covenant represents part of the reaction against this superficiality. It states, 'Evangelism itself is the proclamation of the historical, biblical Christ as Saviour and Lord, with a view to persuading people to come to him personally and so be reconciled to God. In issuing the gospel invitation we have no liberty to conceal the cost of discipleship. Jesus still calls all who would follow him to deny themselves, take up their cross and identify themselves with his new community.'[4]

Jesus himself often spoke of false prophets and a false gospel, warning of those who would be shocked to the core when he disowned them at the Judgment Seat. Perhaps we need to recognise that Christ's right to be Saviour is inextricably linked to his authority as Lord. John Owen, the Puritan preacher once clearly warned, 'You have an imaginary Christ, and if you are satisfied with an imaginary Christ you must be satisfied with an imaginary salvation.'

It is time that Jesus was no longer relegated to the status of simply being known as Saviour. His authority must be shouted from the rooftops. 'Who is this King of glory? The Lord of hosts, he is the King of glory' (Psalm 24:10). My friend and my Saviour has always been, and for ever must be my Lord and my King. It is not within the bounds of eternal possibilities that he can be anything less. It could aptly be said that in this case our heavenly Father is a capitalist – he only believes in take-over bids!

A. W. Tozer, referring to the gospel of his day as 'the discredited doctrines of a divided Christ', commented that it goes like this, 'Christ is both Saviour and Lord. A sinner may be saved by accepting him as Saviour without yielding to him as Lord', and he retorted, 'Christ's Saviourhood is for ever united to his Lordship. Christ must be Lord or he will not be Saviour.'[5]

2. *The 'accepting' Jesus fallacy.* This is the most common error among Bible-believing churches today. The phrase is not biblical – in fact the Bible tells the opposite. The doctrine is summarised in the phrase which so often forms the total content of an evangelistic appeal, 'Accept Jesus as your Saviour'. Not only is this appeal emotive, it is also fallacious. Apart from the fact that Jesus must be Lord in order to be Saviour, the concept of 'accepting' Jesus is ludicrous. It forgets that Jesus Christ – King of Kings, Lord of Lords, the everlasting King of glory, the holy Son of God – cannot just accept you on your terms. Holiness and sin can never walk meekly together. One must always bow to the other. Jesus can only gladly welcome sinners when they come in repentance, seeking forgiveness; never when they expect him to bless them in their sin!

The 'accept' Jesus phrase is totally meaningless when used just as it stands. It is not contained in the Scriptures; and on one occasion when 'accept' is used the question asked is not 'Will you accept Jesus?' but 'Will he accept you?' It is not a case of 'Will the sinner accept the King?' but 'Will the King accept the sinner?'

On one occasion I was speaking to a gathering of preachers on this subject when one of them interrupted from the back saying, 'I don't agree, what about Revelation 3:20?'. This is the classic proof-text for the whole notion of accepting Jesus into your heart. 'Behold I stand at the door and knock; if anyone hears my voice and opens the door I will come in to him and eat with him, and he with me.' But these words were not written to non-Christians. They were addressed to the members of the backslidden church of Laodicea. The picture is not of a weak, feeble Jesus standing at the door of the sinners heart with the dew glistening in his hair, desperately pleading to be allowed to come in. (How easily we forget that the 'Gentle Jesus, meek and mild' we were brought up on is really the King of glory.) Jesus just does not stand and feebly plead. The true picture is that of the Good Shepherd going out and bringing the wanderers back. He goes to find his own backslidden Christians and waits to be allowed to return to his rightful position as Lord and King of their lives.

The famous picture by Holman Hunt which is so often used to illustrate so-called 'deeper points' of Revelation 3:20 has nothing at all to do with it. It was a painting based upon John 8:12, when Jesus said 'I am the Light of the world' and called men to leave their lives and come with him into the light of his life!

Returning to the questioner I added, 'There is only one other argument. The Scriptures can have a dual meaning, so there may be a secondary application for non-christians in Revelation 3:20, but only if it is considered in context. So what is the last word of Revelation 3:19? He could not answer. In fact the word is 'repent' and it is the forgotten word in our evangelistic vocabulary. Our message must never be one of 'easy acceptance' without true repentance and commitment. When Paul talked about accepting, he said, 'I appeal to you therefore, brethren, by the mercies of God, to present your bodies as a living sacrifice, holy and acceptable to God, which is your spiritual worship (Rom. 12:1). Again it is a question of whether he will accept us, and not vice versa. The answer is always 'yes', but on grounds of Jesus' own gospel, denying yourself, taking up your cross, and following him.

Accepting Jesus is only a valid concept when applied to his standards and attributes, not his personality. A whole new generation of Christians has come into contemporary

14

society believing that it is possible to 'accept' Christ without forsaking the world.

Jesus died to show us how to come to God, not just through an easy acceptance of who he is but by crucifixion of the old life and resurrection into the new; taking his lifestyle and knowing it implanted in us.

3. The third problem lies in our *understanding of the word 'believe'*. For years this word conveyed the very heart of the Christian gospel, yet in recent times it has gained a variety of meanings which only lead to confusion. A year or two back I was talking with my father about the meaning of the gospel. He stated firmly 'Believe in the Lord Jesus, and you will be saved' (Acts 16:31). 'What', I asked, 'does believe mean?' 'That's easy,' was the reply. 'It means total and complete surrender of your life to Jesus Christ, recognising he died because he loved you and asking him to share his life with you by living in you as Lord and Saviour.' That answer is, of course, completely correct. But nowadays 'believe' has aquired the general meaning of an intellectual acceptance, a basic recognition of the facts, rather than a commitment of lifestyle. Even the Devil believes there is a God but that hardly makes him a Christian!

It is probably fair to assert that more gospel addresses have been delivered on John 3:16 than on any other verse – 'For God so loved the world that he gave his only son, that whoever believes in him should not perish but have eternal life.' For today's generation that word 'believes' can too easily mean a mental acceptance of the life and death of Jesus. Too many have been led to believe that this theoretical concept is sufficient for conversion and that no radical change of lifestyle or perspective is required. That is not the New Testament position.

Real belief is more than mental acceptance of an historical Jesus or a set of doctrinal propositions, it is the opening of life to Jesus in simple trust and commitment so that he can enter that life and have control and authority

15

there by virtue of his position as the Saviour God and King of Kings. 'In the context of men's relation to God the verb (to believe – pisteuō) always implies a personal conviction and trust arising within a direct personal relationship. The New Testament Greek reflects this point by introducing a preposition ('believe in . . . ') . . . Obedience and conformity to what God prescribes is the inevitable concomitant of believing.'[6]

In the Scriptures the faith which comes from believing is joined together with obedience, and you can always tell true belief because it leads a man to obey Jesus in all his life. For the writers of the New Testament the call to believe was a call to discipleship. It meant total surrender to Jesus with all the ethical demands that involved. It was far more than an intellectual belief in the divinity of Christ or in some doctrine of atonement. David Watson summarises, 'To believe in Jesus Christ involves an active commitment to a person, without knowing where he will lead you, or how he will test you.'[7]

It is always easier to be critical and negative than to be positive and constructive. Yet these three errors have brought us such a bitter harvest that we need to be clear about the imbalance they provoke. Above all we need to regain a balance in our presentation of the gospel between its two major constituents – demand and offer. Of course Christianity involves the 'offer' of resurrection, but it presupposes the 'demand' of being crucified first. For too long we have looked to the offer and denied the demand. We want to be saved, but we stubbornly insist that Christ does all the dying. Instead of leading men to a cross, too often we encourage them to live in the strength of their dying manhood.

An older saint who taught me the truths of the crucified life was once asked by a young Christian, 'What does it mean to be crucified?' The old saint replied that it meant three things – the crucified man is only facing in one direction, he's not going back, and he has no further plans of his own. Our largely uncrucified generation lacks that kind of singlemindedness. If only we stopped looking back longingly at some of the old ways, knew we'd said goodbye to a lost life, and were content with carrying out his plans rather than making our own.

All unannounced and mostly undetected there has come in modern times a new cross into popular evangelical circles.

From this cross has sprung a new philosophy of the Christian life, and from the new philosophy has come a new evangelical technique – a new type of meeting and a new kind of preaching.

The old cross would have no truck with the world. For Adam's proud flesh it meant the end of the journey. The new cross, if understood aright, is the source of oceans of good clean fun and innocent enjoyment. It lets Adam live without interference. His life motivation is unchanged; he still lives for his own pleasure.

The new cross does not slay the sinner, it redirects him. It gears him into a cleaner and jollier way of living and saves his self-respect.

The old cross is a symbol of death. God salvages the individual by liquidating him and then raising him again to newness of life. God offers life, but not an improved old life. The life he offers is life out of death. It stands always on the far side of the cross.[8]

That is the best summary I know of the gospel we are in danger of losing and the terrible price we are paying for losing it. John the Baptist found himself ministering to a very similar society. Israel emphasised offer at the expense of demand. They claimed a pedigree, and suggested that the demand had been so fulfilled by their ancestor Abraham that all that was required of contemporary Israelites was to receive the promises at no extra cost to themselves.

We fall into the very same trap today. So much of our

message emphasises 'offer' because 'demand' would put people off. It is in this area that the evangelist most resembles the door-to-door salesman – 'Do you want love, joy, peace, etc. etc. – come to Jesus.' That can never be the total gospel message. It must be balanced by the demands involved. We have engaged in a subtle sell-out, sacrificing the message of Jesus for the sake of our respectability in the community.

If modern-day evangelists met the rich young ruler he would never have been allowed to walk away. Instead we would run after him and offer 50 per cent or even 10 per cent (the Bible talks much of a tithe!) of his life in return for his decision. We would then consider that he was guaranteed eternal life! Jesus knew that there could be no such compromise – so he simply laid it on the line and told it like it is. We need to balance our casual offer with the demands which Jesus laid down. We need to be true to the Bible and not our evangelical imaginations!

Let's stop making the Christian life so easy that it seems contemptible. Rather than attracting people with our 'easy' gospel we have merely repelled them.

When we regain the message of Jesus, then our country may begin to listen again.

'Whoever does not bear his own cross and come after me, cannot be my disciple . . . whoever of you does not renounce all that he has cannot be my disciple (Luke 14:27, 33).

18

Paradise Now

We want
to zap them
with holiness

We want
to levitate them
with joy

We want
to open them
with love vessels

We want
to clothe the wretched
with linen and light

We want
to put music and truth
in our underwear

We want
to make the land and its cities glow
with creation

We will make it
irresistible
even to racists...

We want to change
the demonic character of our opponents
into productive glory

Julien Beck

2:
God's frozen people

'If I become a Christian does that mean I have to go to church?'

'Why are Christians so divided? Why all those different churches? Why don't Christians get on too well together?'

'Christianity, I'm interested in, but not the church. It's got no credibility.'

No doubt you are only too familiar with these and similar statements. Any kind of involvement with personal witness will mean that you have either heard these comments or others like them. Today's world is utterly alienated from the church. The biggest tragedy is that it is only now as we slowly emerge from our ecclesiastical ice age that we are beginning to realise the extent of our alienation from society. Bishop Stephen Neill summarised it in these words, 'Nothing in the contemporary scene is more striking than the general regard which is felt for Jesus Christ and the general dislike of the organised church which bears his name.'

When Jesus ascended to heaven he took his body with him, but left a different body behind. His church was to be the living body of Christ, the vivid demonstration of the reality of Jesus, the Son of God. We have never had the right to hide the importance of the church and her tragic failure behind the simplistic phrase 'Oh don't look at the church, look at Jesus!' The church was to be the walking, talking, living, breathing demonstration of the glory of the living God – how dare we try to excuse our sorry state with such feeble excuses.

'Don't look at the church, look at Jesus' really does represent the easy way out. Even as we utter it we are guilty of denying our responsibility as God's ambassadors to a hostile country. Unfortunately it is a reply that has been endorsed by useage and hallowed by tradition; it also reveals a very sorry truth. Worst of all it is sin. We stand condemned out of our own mouths by denying, or writing off, the very body and bride of Jesus. We open ourselves up to his judgment. Perhaps we have forgotten that we too are part of the church. We too make up part of that bride of Christ along with everyone who has come into a living encounter with a Jesus who now reigns as Lord and King in their lives. In dismissing the church's effectiveness as a witnessing expression of the beauty of Jesus, we dismiss ourselves at the same time.

Step inside the terminal ward of any city hospital for just a moment. Consider the woman lying prostrate on the hospital bed, incapable of movement, her body racked with pain. Her body is emaciated, eaten away by cancer within, slowly growing weaker and approaching death. Now think of her as your mother, your sister, or your wife. That blood relationship remains as real as when you first knew her, basically unaltered by the presence of this ghastly disease. Only the context in which that relationship can be carried on has been radically changed.

Similarly, the church, even in her present state, remains the bride of Christ. However, the difference lies in the fact that her healing is not merely a possibility, it is a divine certainty, underwritten by God himself. One day the glorious, risen Jesus is returning for a final visit to planet Earth, and he's coming back to get married! That end-time wedding will not feature the bride as a dirty, haggard, feeble old woman but a triumphant, victorious, renewed and revived bride, fit for the King whose love has restored her.

God's end-time purpose as a loving Father was never to bring you (singular) to him, but us (plural) together into an eternity of knowing and loving him. Yet we have gone and told needy people not to look at the living, dynamic family of God but to some Sunday school memory of an ethereal Jesus who will forgive them and come into their hearts. Or we have successfully filtered the biblical gospel of all unpleasant content so that all we are left with is a rude spiritual survival kit. All this does is preserve as much of my old lifestyle as is possible without losing my new-found place in the future heavenly kingdom. Then we wonder why so many of our spiritual babies are still-born!

What a tragic distortion!

Admittedly, the spirit of the age is individualistic but it was never meant to contaminate the church. When Jesus comes to our lives it is not simply with a bargain package promising forgiveness, reconciliation and eternal life. He comes to take up residence as Lord and King and brings with him both his Father and his Spirit. Yet not only does Jesus bring us a spiritual rebirth through a Holy Trinity, we also get introduced into a new family. That is a tie we cannot avoid.

John Wesley was riding on his horse one day when a man rode up alongside. As they talked the man told Wesley a truth he never forgot. 'Sir, you wish to serve God and get to heaven. Remember, you'll never get there alone. You must either find companions or make them for the Bible knows nothing of solitary religion.'

Each of us needs something to be converted into. God's answer is his family – what a lovely thought, suddenly we find we have millions of brothers and sisters with whom we are linked to become the bride of Jesus! We were not made to survive alone, together the Lord draws us on to build each other up into full maturity in him.

When I first became a Christian I was very much a 'loner'. I was also spiritually very weak. Even going to theological college made little difference. While in my first year at college my spiritual life was viewed with some confusion by many people. Some caused me real pain by questioning whether or not I was even a Christian. The trouble was I was trying to grow in the Lord on my own, and, worse still, I wasn't getting very far. One evening, as I stood alone washing my socks and underwear in the college basement, a fellow student, all of six feet four inches and a rugby player to boot, joined me to undertake a similar task with his socks. The result? We ended up having a prayer meeting over those socks and for the first time I knew I would never get anywhere with God just on my own.

I thank God for the friendship of John and many others whose fellowship drew me closer to Jesus. The girl I later married was a contemporary of John and I at college. She has a lovely way of describing the results of the sock-washing incident: 'You became two spiritual cripples hobbling along together.' That is not a bad analogy. Neither of us were terribly stable spiritually, but together we could draw each other on. That's the kind of friendship and commitment we all need.

The church was never designed by her Lord to be an institution or a building. She was always intended to be a loving fellowship of brothers and sisters bonded together in Jesus: a living testimony to the way God unites different generations, classes, sexes, characters into a reflection of his power, love and glory. The church is people. People who love Jesus and are committed to one another whatever their denominational label may be. We must constantly remind ourselves that in the first place the church is not any particular denomination or building.

The 1970s saw a new growth of appreciation for one another within the family of God and the beginnings of a new loving attitude which could overcome all the old conflicts. Where the ecumenical movement had failed to bring Christians together on the grounds of reason, frequently the move of the Spirit of God brought a real loving commitment to one another. A new bride could well be in formation – indeed it's enough to make you think the bridegroom could be coming!

Jesus brought his people together for a purpose. He always had an eternal plan and his Church was to play the major role – 'To make all men see what is the plan of the mystery hidden for ages in God who created all things; that through the church the manifold wisdom of God might now be made known to the principalities and powers in the heavenly places. This was according to the eternal purpose' (Eph. 3:9–11). The ultimate goal of the universe is to provide the pure and holy bride of Christ.

In brief, this universe was made as the ideal setting for man to live within, and humanity was created in the image and likeness of God so that mankind could provide a suitable, eternal companion for Jesus. The fall was followed by judgment, flood and then the promise of redemption. The messianic race was born and nurtured to bring in the Messiah. The Messiah came for one reason alone and that was to give birth to his church, to obtain his bride.

> This cosmology asserts that as far as Scripture reveals, all that God has done for all eternity, and all that he will do until the marriage supper of the Lamb, is concerned primarily with one thing, and only one: the gathering out and training of his bride for her exhalted position of co-rulership with the son over his vast, ever-expanding external kingdom in the ages to come. All that precedes the marriage supper of the Lamb for all eternity is only preliminary to God's eternal enterprise. Only after the bride is on the throne with her Lover and Lord will God be ready to unveil his creative programme for the eternal ages.[1]

While we are here in this life we are Christ's body, later

we will reign as his bride and joint heir. In the meantime we have a tremendous responsibility to act and live as the body, but also to complete that body by bringing into kingdom life those that God would add to the church. The church is not just a rest home for convalescence after the problems of the week, it is another name for the pioneer people of the King who have been called out for his purpose.

The church, or *ekklesia*, is the title of the people of God, not merely the name of the building in which they worship. We miss the mark if we see 'church' as just the routine performance of ritual worship in buildings specifically set aside for that purpose. The church is the company of believers, born again, yielded under the Lordship of Christ Jesus and living in vital relationship with him by the Holy Spirit. The church is the name of a family group called for a purpose, travelling to a specific destination to fulfil a glorious role in an eternity of ruling and reigning with her bridegroom. 'The church is the pilgrim people of God. It is on the move – hastening to the ends of the earth to beseech all men to be reconciled to God, hastening to the end of time to meet its Lord who will gather all into one.'[2]

The church and evangelism are indivisibly intertwined. She is God's only agent of evangelism, the sole redeeming agency through which he expresses himself to the world, and evangelism can never be true evangelism unless it is rooted and grounded in the church. As Howard Snyder has publicly stated, 'The church is the only divinely appointed means of spreading the gospel. Evangelism makes little sense divorced from the Christian community. Biblical evangelism is church-centred evangelism. The church is both the agent and the goal of evangelism.'

For an evangelist to isolate himself from the church will always involve a contradiction in terms because non-church-based evangelism cannot be biblical evangelism. Jesus did not call us to create converts within a lonely, individualistic relationship with him but to go and make 'disciples'. To do that must mean that the church is mobilised and involved in every aspect of both our witness and follow-up. If this is so, then why, we must ask ourselves, is so much of our evangelism pinned around the phrase 'come to Jesus' and not 'join his family'? We have made salvation so individualistic and personal that it has lost most of its communal aspects. Many of our hymns reveal this disturbing tendency, all 'I' and 'my' with so few 'we' and 'our' that most of them would be more suitable as solos!

All of this would seem to imply that in many ways evangelism seeks to disown church, yet there is a very different side to the coin. For decades throughout Britain evangelism has taken a back-seat in most church itineraries. Where it has been given a place, only too frequently substandard presentations have lead to its being relegated to the background. Programmes of evangelism are allowed to come and go with the regularity of changing fashions. A radical view of evangelism as an essential part of the life and lifeblood of the church has not been allowed to gain ground. Any concept of the church being involved in every member evangelism is frequently strenuously resisted.

More recently, the much-needed resurgence of emphasis on worship in the church has resulted in a pendulum-like swing against 'service'. Worship is always meant to be the heart-cry of the spirit of mankind to God. A proclamation of love and loyalty which encourages a witness out of which flows praise for all the Lord does, is the response to the natural evangelism of our worshipping hearts. Instead of this dynamic, circular, increasing flow we have fallen into a tragic 'either . . . or' mentality.

Evangelism has too often been looked at as either unnecessary, unspiritual, or the province of professionals alone. Disappointed people with a heart desire to evangelise, rejected by their local fellowship as a little 'too keen' have begun to see and denounce the church as the greatest hindrance to evangelism. Too often such people have turned in frustration to walk alone, or alongside a para-church evangelistic society, simply in the absence of anywhere else to go!

If evangelism is truly to have its beginning and end in the church then attitudes must alter radically. Change cannot be confined to those reluctantly engaged in non-church-based evangelism alone; the body of Christ, the church as a whole, needs again to recognise her God-given function and fulfil the great commission which Jesus laid upon her.

One of the many obstacles lying in her path is the Devil. Satan has always tried to complicate, undermine and then destroy that which the Spirit of God is building. In the field of evangelism he has, initially, been alarmingly successful. The church, in general, has failed to communicate adequately the gospel in Britain for nearly a hundred years. Her failure to reveal Christ has exposed her to ridicule and rejection, causing her to be dismissed as the grey Gothic building on the street corner, a source of architectural interest, but little else. This was always Satan's intention.

Ever since his dramatic defeat on a tiny hill, outside a small city, in an insignificant country under an occupied power, when the Son of God suffered on a simple wooden cross, Satan has known that his only avenue of attack lay within the church. 'Satan cannot prevent Jesus returning for his people, resplendent with personal glory. Therefore enemy activity is concentrated against the church. His plan is that Christ, on returning, will find nothing but a prostituted bride, a body full of sickness and the ruins of a building.'[3] To achieve these ends Satan has utilised three major weapons – traditionalism, institutionalism and isolationism.

Unless the church of Christ in twentieth-century Britain can rise up, like Lazarus, into the resurrection life which

28

is her birthright in Jesus; unless she can be delivered from the fetters of tradition, institutionalism and lack of love, she will never be ready to face her bridegroom. These things are guarded so jealously, and they strangle the church in her very birth-pangs. Evangelism has properly been described as, 'that which removes the hindrances in the church to growth'. Perhaps that explains why the church pays only lip-service to the vision of outreach and mission. Perhaps whole-hearted evangelism would be too dangerous!

I have always found it very significant that when an unchurched business or professional man commits his life to Jesus Christ and joins a church, sparks often fly. He will frequently exhibit an impatience and frustration normally reserved for business competitors. He seems incapable of understanding why we have produced so many obstacles as barriers to our communication. Our structure and traditions seem to him to hinder our message rather than promote it.

If we were to step back in time through to the first years of the Christian church we would discover that evangelism in the early church was not all mass-meetings. The gospel spread like wildfire simply because it was 'gossipped' in the market places of the world. Anointed apostolic preaching came a poor second in Middle Eastern communications. It was the natural everyday witness of each born-again child of God which set up the chain reaction by which the early church grew.

Personal witness did not just mean that the church grew in quantity (or obesity), it also grew in quality of lifestyle (that's maturity), because the world was watching. They longed to share Jesus with their friends and contemporaries. Nothing came more naturally than sharing the good news of what Jesus had done in their lives, and then living in such a way that people couldn't help noticing how the relationship was growing! This was, and is, true evangelism. The gospel just becomes an explanation of our lifestyle, a lifestyle which is so striking that it stops people in their tracks. The crowds were amazed when Peter began the pattern: 'For these men are not drunk . . . but this is what was spoken by the prophet Joel' (Acts 2:15–16). It is a sad commentary on the church of Christ in this land that no one would ever suppose we were anything but stone-cold sober.

We might well ask when God's chosen people reverted to being his frozen people. Despite brief periods when the church has been vibrant and alive, church history generally is not a triumphal story. It would not be so bad if persecution had started the downhill trend, but instead, throughout history, wherever the church has faced militant opposition she has grown in strength and numbers. Tertullian, the second-century Christian historian shrewdly commented, 'The blood of the martyrs is the seed of the church.' Familiar scenes come to mind. The elderly Bishop of Smyrna, Polycarp, a well-respected member of the community was urged by the Roman Governor to renounce Christ and save himself from death. His reply: 'For eighty and six years have I been his servant, and he has done me no wrong, and how can I blaspheme my King who saved me.' The Romans burnt him, but Polycarp and thousands like him gave to the church some of her most glorious chapters of expansion and growth.

The development of gospel proclamation was never halted by persecution. Nor did evangelism cease because the world was converted and therefore there was no further need. Instead, the reason was far more insidious and lies in the heart of man himself. Mankind has a secret desire to be accepted, to be popuar and respectable. Slowly, as the centuries passed the church's great betrayal grew more and more obvious. Instead of standing out as a radical, alternative society the church conformed in increasing measure to the standards of the day, and where biblical truth got in the way it was quietly ignored. Instead of converting the world, the world converted the church;

compromise grew into carnality; and the church grew fat and contented. The effects on evangelism were frightening. 'Sin' became almost a forbidden subject and the concept of disturbing either nominal Christianity or worldly indifference was frowned upon.

Today's world with its surfeit of broken congregations and broken clergy bears eloquent testimony to the manner in which the living, vital body of Christ has been distorted into an inflexible institution crippling to evangelism. God is always moving on, but he seeks to take his people with him. We don't want change for the sake of it. The traditions of the elders cannot be lightly dismissed, but they must be sacrificed if we are failing to be relevant in today's world. David Winter once wrote, 'In the institutional, moribund, introverted ranks of our Christian churches, we have a private dialogue with ourselves while man plunges suicidally on into absurdity and despair.'

This book is written in the light of the changes which God is introducing into his church. Changes are taking place in structure, message, desire and hope which only serve to illustrate the tremendous potential which exists among us all. Some months ago I had the privilege of going with Graham Kendrick to conduct a weekend of ministry at a church in a working class mining town in the North-East of England. We went knowing nothing of the situation. Imagine our amazement at discovering a church which has to meet in the National Union of Mineworkers hall because it has outgrown everywhere else; a church where the evening service began at seven p.m. and ended around ten-thirty p.m.; a church where the service had to be stopped after five minutes so that more chairs could be brought in to seat those queuing outside; a church where all Sunday afternoon direct communication took place with un-churched people and even after two hours of that, the pre-service Prayer Meeting was absolutely packed to the doors! Is it any wonder that 200 people have been added to the church and that non-Christians gladly come out of real interest to discover what could have changed the lives of their friends? The real miracle is that all this happened because seventeen people started praying and dreaming together. God has done it before and he can do it again.

Traditionalism and institutionalism have reigned in our churches for far too long. We have unthinkingly gone on doing things in a particular way for no better reason than that is the way we've always done it! Motivated more by love for our own comfort and security than for a world lost without Jesus we have become increasingly isolated – doing our own thing while the world has tended to look on in faint amusement. Attempts at change and reform have come and gone; gimmicks have been introduced and discarded; change brought in but only for the sake of change. Then something new began. In the aftermath of a crumbling ecumenical movement God began to teach his people what it really meant to love one another. From this came a new spirit of enquiry. Perhaps we had forgotten other things as well.

Natural changes have begun because we serve a God who once said 'Behold, I make all things new' (Rev. 21:5). When the church starts to ask, 'What does God want in this situation?' then change becomes inevitable. 'Every age knows the temptation to forget that the gospel is ever new. We try to contain the new wine of the gospel in old wineskins – outmoded traditions, obsolete philosophies, creaking institutions, old habits. But with time the old wineskins begin to bind the gospel. Then they must burst, and the power of the gospel pour forth once more.'[4]

If the church in the last quarter of the twentieth century is to recover from the sins and omissions of the first three-quarters, then a new vision must emerge. We need to see the development of new attitudes and a new desire in a renewed church.

God can only fully move through evangelism in this land when the complete church of his Son is prepared to provide a family for people to be converted into and a living testimony to the indwelling Jesus which the watching world can see! At the same time a real openness must be seen in structures and concepts so that the total gospel can be communicated to the total world. The church should never require apology, only explanation.

At that time a new day can start to dawn in the church. When loving communities start to march again as the pioneer people of God – then the world will tremble and the citadels of Satan fall. Then the people of God can return to the old way, to live again as the children of the King. J.B. Phillips summarised that 'old way' in these words which he used to describe why the Spirit of God used the early church to turn their world upside down: 'Perhaps because of their very simplicity, perhaps because of their readiness to believe, to obey, to give, to suffer, and if need be to die, the Spirit of God found what he must always be seeking – a fellowship of men and women so united by love and faith that he can work in them and through them with the minimum of hindrance.'⁵

Then, and only then, will the whole land hear and see the glory of the Lord. Then, and only then, will the waiting bridegroom come and claim his bride to reign with him throughout eternity.

And he said to me, 'Son of man, can these bones live?' And I answered, 'O Lord God, thou knowest.' . . . Then he said to me . . . 'I will put my Spirit within you, and you shall live, and I will place you in your own land; then you shall know that I, the Lord, have spoken, *and I have done it* (Ezek. 37:3, 14).

All

I heard a priest, one who lived the Gospel, preach the
  Gospel.
The humble, the poor, were carried away,
The prominent, the wealthy, were shocked,
And I thought that such preaching of the Gospel
would soon frighten away many of those now filling
the church, and attract those now shunning it.

It occurred to me that it is a bad sign for a follower
of Christ to be well thought of by conventional 'Christians'.
Rather, it would be better if we were singled out as crazy
  or radical.
It would be better if they pursued us, signed petitions
against us, tried to get rid of us.

This evening, Lord, I'm afraid.
I am afraid, for your Gospel is terrible.
It is easy to hear it preached,
It is relatively easy not to be shocked by it,
But it is very difficult to live it . . .

. . . I should give everything,
I should give everything till there is not a single
pain, a single misery, a single sin in the world.

I should then give all, Lord, all the time.
I should give my life.

Lord it is not true, is it?
It is not true for everyone.
I am exaggerating, I must be sensible!
Son, there is only *one* commandment,
For *everyone*:
You shall love with *all* your heart,
                with *all* your soul,
                with *all* your strength.

Michel Quoist

3:
. . . And you love your secret Saviour

He was made with the highest destiny in the universe. Each blueprint was only used once, and then discarded. Uniquely designed to know and love God with the glorious freedoms of individuality and personality. Made in the image of God – we may well be permitted to ask – 'What happened to the human race?'

G. K. Chesterton once wrote, 'We have all read about the man who has forgotten his name. The man walks about the streets and can see and appreciate everything, only he cannot remember who he is. Well everyman is like that in the story.'

Self-satisfied, yet strangely frustrated at losing the direction of his destiny, modern man goes on asking the questions of life and the questions of death without ever being quite sure where the answers lie. It is so tragic that the grey, Gothic building on the street corner is associated in the popular imagination with decay and death when it alone has the message of life! 'Today there is no shortage of critics who take delight in caricaturing and knocking the church. TV and radio have firmly established the image of the ecclesiastical as eccentric, insipid little men surviving in a fantasy world of their own, the quaint relics of some bygone age, answering incomprehensibly the questions that no one is asking.'[1]

We have the most wonderful task in this world today –

our task is to communicate the living Christ to dying men in such a way that they may turn from death to life. We are like a bent-up, crippled arthritic who, having discovered a cure and become healthy, refused to share that cure with others. Once we have received Jesus' offer of life, we are committed to relay that to others. We must face the searching question – Why have we failed to fulfil his great commission? Jesus said, 'Go therefore and make disciples of all nations' because 'all authority in heaven and on earth has been given to me' (Matt. 28:18–19). Yet, we have dismissed the command because it has been inconvenient and we have failed to communicate to a lost world the fabulous offer of Jesus.

We could never say that the message was incomplete because the quality of the offer that Jesus makes is quite incredible. He never offered an easy life, nor an automatically happy one, but he does offer personal forgiveness and reconciliation to God: a real atonement and justification; plus redemption from the slavery of an old life into a very different lifestyle. These realities of the faith are not rooted in more subjective experiences but in objective, historical events. Jesus is no mere 'trip'. He lived, died and rose again in our world, during our history and proved his divine status in a way no other prophet has ever been able to emulate. The offer is genuine and the resurrection proved it. Faith has to play its part because resurrection can never be logically proven, but it is worth noting that the idea that Christianity has a rational basis has in the last decade received a great deal of support from contemporary apologetics.

Jesus brings a genuine offer of forgiveness, justification and new life. These are terms that we can be so familiar with and yet that very familiarity can lead to a failure to grasp the full implications of all that is being held out to us. With that in mind let us look at them more precisely.

1. *Forgiveness* – not just in terms of an easy passing over of sin, but a total clearing of the record. The cross

was absolutely central to God's plans. It was never God's intention that patched-up guilt-ridden lives should be presented as a bride for his only son. It was always the Father's intention that total condemnation would be removed by an unparalleled sacrifice. So the Son of God had to die on a Roman gibbet, near a Jerusalem rubbish dump, in order that the world might gain freedom from the law of sin and death. By this event rooted in human history, the power of the Devil was permanently crippled and all who would acknowledge a new King in Jesus were brought back to God.

Sacrifice has always had to involve the spilling of innocent blood. Through the death of Jesus the sin which had separated man and God since the Fall was removed and reconciliation achieved; through the blood of Jesus the realities of sin are removed. But is that sufficient for the restoration of the complete man because surely the past remains?

When I was a boy, having been brought up in a Christian home, I had gained a picture of the Second Coming of Jesus. I didn't suffer from the kind of paranoid fear that my wife remembers. She recalls how as a child she would hear a large articulated lorry change gear outside her home in the middle of the night and panic with fear that the Lord was coming back when she wasn't ready! But one thing did worry me. I could imagine Jesus in heaven with all the Christians gathered round him listening as he read from a big, black book. This book contained the full, unexpurgated biographies of everyone there. What terrified me was the thought of Jesus reading out all my past sins and my father hearing all the things he had never known about! It's a good job that my heavenly Father is just not like that. Not only has the blood of Jesus earned my forgiveness but it has also taken away from the memory of God the very thought of it. The only one who remembers what I was like is *me*, and Jesus seeks even to heal my memory of that too!

We need to remember as we condemn ourselves that the forgiveness of God is supernatural and that the blood of Jesus cleanses us from all the wrong we have done. Even under the old covenant God promised, 'I will forgive their iniquity, and I will remember their sins no more' (Jer. 31:34) and 'thou hast cast all my sins behind thy back' (Isa. 38:17) was the joyful reply. It should be ours as well.

2. *Justification* – a long word which my old theology lecturer used to explain simply as 'being made just as if I had never sinned'. Paul argued out this whole doctrine in Romans 1–8. Fifteen hundred years later Martin Luther read his words and was converted. Simply stated: when we were obviously guilty before God of misusing and abusing our lives, Jesus received our condemnation so that before the throne of God for eternity his blood cries 'Not Guilty' on our behalf. Because we have been acquitted in God's court of law, as it were, we can have 'peace with God' – we are reconciled to him.

3. *New Life* – a completely different lifestyle and a totally new power to live it with. Many Christians get confused with the idea that all Jesus left us was a new and more difficult set of rules and regulations to live by, whereas, in fact, he left us his Spirit who actually wants to live through us. All the functions of the Godhead are dynamic not static, on-going not just occasional. As Dwight L. Moody once said, 'A great many people are trying to make peace, but that has already been done. God has not left it for us to do; all we have to do is to enter into it.' God provides the power, all we need to do is to allow his spirit to enter and live in us as the director of our lives. From our submission and obedience he will work a miracle of grace giving us power to work the unworkable and live the unlivable.

It was for that reason Jesus died. Man is held captive by sin with all its consequences. Jesus gave himself – in a way illustrated by so many modern hi-jackings – as a hostage that we might be set free. So my ransom has been

39

paid and I can live as a perfectly free man. My complete new life came from his complete death on a cross – and from the fact that he rose again and lives in men and women today. The old died on a cross with Jesus, the new has come.

Everything that had been promised to the Jews under the old covenant, had they been obedient, is now to be fulfilled in the people of the new covenant. We are to be the inheritors of the promise of God, joint heirs with Jesus of his Father's kingdom, the bride of the son! That is the offer but the demands are equally real, our life must be changed.

John the Baptist first brought the message. He came calling men to repent and prepare the way of the Lord. In those days when a king went on a journey the road was often specially built: we are called to get a road ready so that it is fit for our King. The call to repentance was a simple call to get lives fit for Jesus to come to. John's message was so simple and straightforward, he told men and women, religious leaders and ordinary people alike that it was useless depending on heritage or tradition. He simply said 'You're dirty, come and get washed – it won't actually make you clean but it will show God that you mean business. He is sending someone else just behind me and when he washes you, then you'll really be clean' (cf. Matt. 3).

Jesus continued the theme. He called men to 'deny themselves': no longer to live self-centred lives, but to be prepared to take second place; 'to take up the cross'; to embrace the realities of suffering for the sake of Jesus; to die to themselves that they might live only to him. (Often Jesus would point out the relevant areas involved in repentance for a person e.g. Zacchaeus and the rich young ruler.) Then Jesus called them to 'follow him', a following that needed to be unreserved and whole-hearted because though God will save a man, he will never save a man and his idol. The message was strong, radical and clear as men turned unhappily away. Jesus always demanded a response that would be rooted not just in the intellect but in the realities of personal experience.

It is that call to an 'old fashioned' radical discipleship which we have lost in the glitter and glamour, tinsel and trappings of the twentieth century. The call to lose your life so that you might find it again as it really should be has been laid to one side by an anxious, struggling church.

We have tried to dismiss it as a call out of the past, yet the character of a holy God is one thing that never changes. Martin Luther once put it like this: 'God creates out of nothing. Therefore until a man is nothing, God can make nothing out of him.' In that lies one of the profoundest truths of the gospel. In that one sense God is a capitalist: he is only involved in takeover bids and he will never be content to share control of a life. His character is that of Lord alone!

If modern man is to turn back to God, he must first hear and see the message of God reflected through God's servants. We have no right to try to fob him off with a pseudo-gospel. We have made the message so insipid and sugary that we believe it should be palatable to anyone. Instead, such prostitution of the gospel has created mass-nausea. If the church is to regain her authority she must no longer refer to 'moral dilemma' but 'sin', not 'accept' but 'repent'. She must reveal God as a holy God and man as a hopeless sinner. We must return in penitence and humility to the truth, so that the King may rule, and the kingdom may come. Jesus brought 'good news', but it was good news of a King and a kingdom. He brought life, but at the price of a cross. He called men but demanded everything – that message is one that we will never have the right not to communicate to our world, or to our generation.

It is very easy to excuse ourselves. The reasons roll off our tongues. Yet evangelism was never meant to be the task of a professional élite – it is still the call of God to all of his people. Now that is not meant in any way to deny the ministry of the evangelist (as an evangelist myself I could scarcely do that). It is however designed to point out that each one of us has a God-designed role to play in evangelism today. By no means am I trying to suggest that we should all leave our employment to become involved in so-called 'full time Christian service' – our secular work can be as full time for God and far more effective than most of us realise. Nor am I trying to suggest that each one of us should be shouting the gospel from the rooftops – perhaps only one in ten of us will have that kind of proclamatory ministry. But there are three basic categories of evangelistic involvement and none of these can be independent or exclusive of the others. Nor can any one claim to be superior. 'The eye cannot say to the hand "I have no need of you" . . . On the contrary the parts of the body which seem to be weaker are indispensable' (I Cor. 12:21–2).

The witness

This is the basic calling for today's Christian: ' "You are my witnesses" says the Lord, "and my servant whom I have chosen" ' (Isa. 43:10). We were made to be mugs – or vessels, pots, containers – in whom, and through whom our indwelling Lord can express his glory.

The chief function of the witness is to direct attention away from himself and towards somebody else who is generally neither recognised nor understood. When Jesus came he was not recognised by the people. John the Baptist superbly illustrates the role of the witness in the case of Jesus. Even standing with his closest associates John points out Jesus – 'Behold the Lamb' – and quietly stands by as his disciples leave him to follow Jesus, proclaiming that the popularity of Jesus makes him supremely happy because it fulfils the function for which he was sent. John died a lonely man, denouncing the immorality of a king, and having lived his life as a signpost proudly proclaiming

– 'Don't look at me, look at Jesus.' He pronounced his own epitaph, the tribute of a witness, 'He must increase, but I must decrease.'

Our call to be witnesses involves both gain and loss. We must lose enough of our own self-centred lifestyle that the beauty of Jesus may fill our lives and flow out in observable fashion. The problem is that so often we are too full of ourselves, our own priorities and ambitions, our own anxieties and fears, that there is no room left in our lives through which the Lord can live and express his lifestyle. We become so filled with our needs and problems that there is nothing about our lives which would stop people in their tracks. 'Too many of the called-out people do not behave like called-out people . . . The lack of love in the church, the lack of fruit for God, the lack of spiritual power, is not because believers are rebellious. They are not bad, or wrong, or naughty, it is . . . because they are babies.'²

This failure to grow which afflicts vast numbers of individual Christians in this country has crippled the church. We have increasingly had to fall back on words with which to speak in order to excuse our lack of right living. If our lives were living witnesses then all our words would need to be but an explanation of our lifestyles.

Some years ago I was preaching on the Welsh border in a small country chapel. Sitting half way back was an elderly gentleman, presumably in his late seventies or early eighties. As I began to talk about Jesus he began to smile. The more I shared, the more he smiled! That smile really said something, it was as if he was saying – 'You're talking about my Jesus. You're talking about the one I've known and loved for fifty years.' His face just glowed – I nearly stopped talking to ask him to join me at the front because his face spoke volumes.

When I was nineteen I met Jesus. Not because of what I heard, but because of what I saw in the life of a young evangelist – he brought me face to face with Jesus.

Before evangelism can be really effective the church must be a witnessing family bearing testimony through transformed lives to the indwelling presence of Jesus. On the day of Pentecost Peter announced 'This is that' and proceeded to explain how transformed lives had been changed by Jesus. All that his words had to be were an explanation of their lifestyle and 3,000 were converted.

The call to be witnesses is a call to demonstrate the life and love of Jesus in the way we have care and compassion for others, in the way we take time to help and listen, in the way we demonstrate our commitment to fellow Christians, in the way we are not ashamed to talk about our Lord, in the expression on our faces, the way we handle our school, college or employment and the way we treat our families – in the love that we show and the people that we are. Christianity can never be confined to what we say and believe; always be what we *do* and *are*! To be a witness must never be limited to the things that we don't do. Instead of Christianity being seen in terms of a bunch of negatives it must be a positive alternative lifestyle which defies explanation in any terms other than that life which states 'Jesus lives here'.

A few years ago in a provincial university I saw a young Jewish girl commit her life to Jesus Christ. Some weeks later one of the non-Christians was talking to a member of the Christian Union, unfortunately quite an unusual occurrence in itself! The non-Christian guy was expressing his surprise and delight at the way in which this girl's life had changed – the freshness, spontaneity and gaiety, the way she kept on talking about Jesus. Just one thing puzzled him – why aren't the rest of you like that? That girl was a tremendous embarrassment to her Christian Union until they too discovered what it means to be a witness.

The workman

I once read this epitaph to a long-dead British Prime

Minister: 'He oiled the wheels so that the machinery of government could go on.' A fine tribute to a man who, though overshadowed by the natural brilliance of many of his colleagues, made the job of successful government possible because he supplied the foundation for and consolidation of the efforts of others.

Today, in the church of Christ, we need to rediscover the value of the spiritual artisan. For too long we have worshipped at the throne of natural gift rather than that of disciplined spirituality. The so-called stars in our Christian galaxy – the current musician, actor or preacher – have spluttered into fitful flame for a few years and then passed into obscurity. Often no living testimony is left behind, because little or nothing of lasting value was achieved. Records were produced, books were sold, major performances given, the crowd went away happy but all for little eternal result. In many ways this could be paralleled to a massive firework display – the artificial brightness glitters and dies while the crowd watches on.

The tragedy lies in the spiritual 'groupies' who worship their heroes and long to be like them, and in the 'heroes' whose premature exposure to the applause of the church causes an equally premature spiritual decline. Everyone suffers and in the long run few are blessed.

God is not seeking superstars. History does not concern the divine search for an individual. Rather it is about the longings of a King for a people. Jesus never chose the kind of disciples that we would have selected for him. He never hunted out the popular or the influential – they only came seeking for Jesus by night, like Nicodemus, or were turned sadly away, like the rich young ruler appalled at the cost of discipleship. Instead Jesus chose simple, ordinary humble folk whose lives were open to be changed and transformed by his Holy Spirit. Natural gift is not always to be coveted, sometimes it can obstruct the operation of the Holy Spirit in the life of the believer. Sometimes, of course, God does take hold of a Saul of Tarsus on a Damascus road

45

but then he often deals with him for years in the desert before releasing him into his lifetime's ministry.

Most of us have no outstanding natural abilities. We will never score the winning goal in the FA Cup Final, make a killing on the Stock Market, play in the Wimbledon final, make a hit record or preach to thousands – but we were made to be God's workmen and that is a far greater honour. However we may feel, none of us is useless when our lives are relaxed in the arms of the living God. Our opportunities for service can be incalculable when we catch sight of all those things which we could allow the Lord to use in us.

1. *Hospitality* – opening our homes, beds and larders to the needs of others, particularly those who are lonely or depressed.

2. *Practical skills* – using our individual abilities to serve one another or the church as a whole e.g. in secretarial work, photography, car mechanics, accounting etc.

3. *Social involvement* – in the work of the local council, in community relations, in various charitable associations or voluntary care services.

4. *Administration* – co-ordinating missions, special events or the work of a local evangelist.

5. *Finance* – giving our money to support the work of God in our country, our church and our world – not just giving a little but tithing what we earn to God. After all, if God gave you ten times what you give to him, could you live on it?

6. *Sharing* – either in our home, club, on the streets or in our churches. Taking the time to talk to others about Jesus.

7. *Helps* – running a Christian book-lending service, baby sitting, caring for the elderly, hospital visitation, lending your car – there is so much which can come from just putting others first.

8. *Prayer* – not just a snatched five minutes but pouring out our hearts to God for our friends, relatives and our

country. At a time when nights or half nights of prayer are being used all over the country a new realisation is dawning of the truth of Leonard Ravenhill's words that in the spiritual battle prayer holds a unique place, but 'never has so much been left by so many to so few'.

9. *Outreach to neighbours* – using our homes as a focal point for reaching our neighbours and our contemporaries. Creating within our homes such an atmosphere of peace which will bear witness to Jesus and provide a base for us to give counsel, help, advice and guidance to others.

10. *Encouragement* – learning how to build each other up. It really is so easy to be negative, to allow our personal jealousy to direct our tongues. Instead of seeking to encourage one another we so often exercise a ministry of discouragement, and so achieve Satan's purposes for him!

We all have different gifts; God's call is to each one of us to make use of the gifts he has entrusted to us. 'We are one body in union with Christ, and we are all joined to each other as different parts of one body. So we are to use our different gifts in accordance with the grace that God has given us' (Rom. 12:5–6, TEV).

It is so easy to despise what we have been given and long to be like others, but that is nothing more than a recipe for disaster. A friend of mine used to spend an evening each week speaking in the open air on a street corner. This was a role for which he, and indeed most working with him, had little enthusiasm and still less ability. They were motivated by a stringent sense of loyalty but were tragically miscast. Some time ago he was asked to arrange a number of meetings and administration was his speciality. So he accepted the task. A speaker was booked, thousands attended and hundreds were spoken to. Open-air work no longer occupies such a high place in his order of priorities – when we find what God has gifted us to do then we should go out and do it, even if it means putting down other jobs.

How often I hear the cry 'I have no time'. Closer enquiry so often reveals so many jobs being done – Sunday school teaching, pastoral work, door to door visitation, etc. All being undertaken with little enthusiasm or ability under the pressure of unspoken spiritual blackmail – 'If you don't do it then we will have to close the work down.' In the absence of a call from God we still so often go ahead because we can see no alternative. How foolish! Our God reigns and he is not utterly dependent on you! If he calls you to a task he will equip you for it, but no call means no divinely aided ability and the absence of that so often means failure. Failure to interest, to communicate, to envision, to impart anything from God. We have done what we conceive to be our duty – but at what cost! God's workman is the man who finds out only what the Lord would have him do, and then pours his heart and life into it.

'Do your best to present yourself to God as one approved, a workman who has no need to be ashamed, rightly handling the word of truth' (2 Tim. 2:15).

A warrior

Some years ago when Billy Graham was holding a crusade in Los Angeles one clergyman complained that his style of evangelism had done serious damage, setting the church back a hundred years. Asked for his reaction, the evangelist wryly replied, 'If that's true then I have failed. What I had hoped we might do is set the church back two thousand years.'

The area in which I personally would most like to see that occur is in the matter of leadership. There seem to be three differences between our practice of selecting leaders today and that of the early church.

1. *We look for natural ability – but they looked for an endowment of power,* for men set apart by the Holy Spirit for the work of ministry. Not just men who thought that they could do the job, but men whose ministry was recognised by others. 'While they were worshipping the Lord

and fasting, the Holy Spirit said, "Set apart for me Barnabas and Saul for the work to which I have called them." Then after fasting and praying they laid their hands on them and sent them off" (Acts 13:2–3).

2. *We look for qualifications – but they looked for spiritual maturity.* Yes, of course, ability and qualifications are important, but how much more important is it for us to have spiritual leaders who are 'men of good repute, full of the Spirit and of wisdom' (Acts 6:3).

3. *We look for men with personal charisma and following – they looked for men whose lifestyles were consistent and disciplined.* Men who were the same in the quietness and privacy of their own homes as they were when ministering to the people.

> Appoint elders . . . if any man is blameless, the husband of one wife, and his children are believers and not open to the charge of being profligate or insubordinate. For a bishop, as God's steward, must be blameless; he must not be arrogant or quick-tempered or a drunkard or violent or greedy for gain, but hospitable, a lover of goodness, master of himself, upright, holy, and self controlled; he must hold firm to the sure word as taught, so that he may be able to give instruction in sound doctrine and also to confute those who contradict it. (Titus 1:5-9)

It is so easy to decry those standards as being too severe – but they are the biblical ones and who are we to settle for less? Our leaders should not be chosen by appointment or popular acclaim but out of genuine recognition that they warrant the title 'men, or women, of God'. If the warrior class of feudal days was weak and inept then society was ripe for conquest and so it is in the church today.

The two main errors that we fall into are looking to the wrong people for leadership and failing to honour those anointed by God for spiritual leadership. This is most obvious in our local situations. It is so easy for familiarity to breed such contempt that we fail to give submission and honour to our local clergy, elders and leaders whom God has placed in authority over us. If we have a right to expect them to give us guidance from God rather than intrusive human wisdom then they have a right to expect our commitment and support.

Today we so easily create our own heroes. A man has an attractive personality, an honest face, he is musically skilled – the next moment he is being moulded by clever, articulate men into becoming a 'superstar' for Jesus. He plays to thousands, his words are treasured, his comments reported, he becomes the apostle of our generation. Yet so often, inside rests a weak frightened personality longing to develop a deeper relationship with God but attracted by the popularity and glamour, manipulated by recording companies or management into pretending to be a spiritual giant. Advertising and publicity perpetuate the myth, and very few observe the reality backstage. To his manager he is a property, to the recording company a musician, to himself an artist, to the churches booking him he is 'in ministry', and to the audience a communicator or an evangelist. Everyone has their own expectation and many leave dissatisfied – but the next recorded disc or the final encore will restore the façade. The pressure is enormous, the problems are probably insoluble until we realise that musicians are Christians involved in entertainment and/or communication who may well be no more spiritually mature than the next person.

None of this is meant to be a specific knock at musicians – much the same could be said of preachers, poets, actors. The difficulty lies in the fact that, as has so often been said, it is almost impossible to get anybody to attend a meeting today where the only attraction is God.

Perhaps the removal of commercialism and profit motive, the diminishing of personal ego, and rationalisation of mass-advertising without the accompaniment of loss of standards or 'professionalism' in the real sense of the word would help. Perhaps a growth of emphasis on prayer rather than performance and the involvement of the many rather than a professional élite would aid us. In addition a clearer understanding is needed of the difference between evangelism, ministry to Christians, and entertainment; along with an appreciation of the importance of all three in their individual ways. When entertainment no longer masquerades as evangelism or vice versa then no longer will we be guilty of self-deception or deceiving others. Then indeed the Christian Entertainment Agency and the Christian Evangelistic Society can happily co-exist side by side with each performing its own function. In this way churches will know that their major evangelistic outreach of the year will not degenerate into mere entertainment. Nor will an event designed to relax and entertain Christians be plagued with guilt that it should be doing more. In calling entertainment – *entertainment;* ministry to Christians – *ministry to Christians;* and evangelism – *outreach* or *evangelism* we will at last be being honest.

For the 1980s we need leadership called out by God, envisioned by him, warriors who know exactly where they are going.

If the church in the second half of this century is to recover from the injuries she suffered in the first half, there must appear a new type of preacher. The proper ruler of the synagogue type will never do. Neither will the priestly type of man who carries out his duties, takes his pay and asks no questions, nor the smooth talking pastoral type who knows how to make the Christian religion acceptable to everyone. All these have been tried and found wanting. Another kind of religious leader must arise among us. He must be of the old prophet type, a man who has seen visions of God and has heard a voice from the throne.[3]

As the Lord prepares his church for service each of us is important. It is exactly because each of us is different that

51

each of us is needed. Before the judgment seat of Christ the warrior will not appear as superior to the workman or the witness, just different, in that he will be called to account for other things. Some of us will be all three at the same time, others, only one. Our roles are different, but our purpose is the same. It must always be to love our Lord, to share the good news of what he can mean to men and women, and to be ready for his return.

It's what we were made for!

Jesus said, 'Blessed are those servants whom the master finds awake when he comes; truly, I say unto you, he will gird himself and have them sit at table, and he will come and serve them' (Luke 12:37).

Battle hymn

There's a sound on the wind like a victory song
Listen now let it rest on your soul
It's a song that I learned from a heavenly King
It's the song of a Battle Royal

Come on heaven's children the city is in sight
There will be no sadness on the other side

There's a loud shout of victory that leaps from our hearts
As we we wait for our conquering King
There's a triumph resounding from dark ages past
To the victory song we now sing

Come on heaven's children the city is in sight
There will be no sadness on the other side

There'll be crowns for the conquerors and white robes to
    wear
There will be no more sorrow or pain
And the battles of earth shall be lost in the sight
Of the glorious Lamb that was slain

Now the King of the Ages approaches the earth
He will burst through the gates of the sky
And all men shall bow down to his beautiful name
We shall rise with a shout we shall fly!

Graham Kendrick

4:
Battle royal

I have nothing to offer but blood, toil, tears and sweat.
You ask, What is our policy? I will say: It is to wage
war, by sea, land and air, with all our might and with all
the strength that God can give us . . . You ask, What is
our aim? I can answer in one word: Victory – victory at
all costs, victory in spite of all terror; victory however
long and hard the road may be.[1]

The people of God were uniquely designed by their creator
to be a pioneer people on the march. They were made to
wage war – total war – with the sole aim of total victory
before them, a victory that their leader made inevitable.
Designed to form the army of God the early church
stormed the strongholds of Satan, released his captives,
resisted the claims of the flesh, and stood before the world
as the living demonstration of the authority and glory of
the King.

From the moment Satan was cast out of heaven in
punishment for his rebellion against divine authority the
world has known no peace. We have suffered, instead, a
fierce and dreadful warfare in which everyone who has
lived and will ever live is automatically involved. This war
moved towards its final phase one Friday afternoon when
a lonely Jew took on the universal powers of darkness

54

and within three days had laid the foundation for a total, crushing victory over the enemy.

Before he died Jesus founded a people who would belong to him – the church. These people, men and women, boys and girls, were never designed to sulk in corners, or to hide in lavish cathedrals, but to live openly before the world. Jesus knew that just by living his lifestyle naturally they would excite the admiration and the violent opposition of mankind. When faced with the church as she is really meant to be the world can never be indifferent, nor the Devil inactive. The great High Priestly prayer of Jesus in John 17 shows that his last thoughts were for the church that would introduce his kingdom to the world, and the world to his kingdom. The war would be long and hard but victory was a cast-iron certainty.

The opening battles of this final offensive went well. Violent persecution failed to stop the people of God; in fact the greater the opposition the more the church grew. She began to symbolise all that Jesus had been, becoming a mirror reflecting this unique lifestyle. Her members lived in mutual love and commitment and the world began to notice. One pagan was recorded to have exclaimed, 'See how these Christians love one another,' and he would only have been one of the many who were stopped in their tracks by this new phenomenon – Christ's own church.

Individual lives were transformed by the Holy Spirit and redirected from self-indulgence into seeking the welfare of others. Society saw changes through the church exercising her positive influence for good. Tens of thousands heard the gospel message, and while thousands were being converted the Devil was most assuredly beating a retreat.

Satan has always been a cunning opponent. When he realised that persecution would never destroy the church, he planned a different campaign against her. We, as the church today, are the living demonstration of his temporary success which has resulted in a major reversal to

55

the ground gained by the first-century Christians. We *know* that Jesus *will* triumph in the end, but an impartial observer looking on at the moment could be forgiven for thinking that a pretty unlikely conclusion to the present state of affairs.

Where persecution could never destroy the church, the enemy employed more subtle means. A cancer has been eating away at the church, with only minor interruption, for sixteen hundred years. The Devil knew that the cancer of institutionalism could compromise truth and turn strong men into cowards. Satan knew that if men of war could be softened by the luxuries of peace time, then they would lose their martial arts and avoid rather than seek conflict. If popularity could be made to be more palatable than integrity, then men who would once have shouted the truth might relapse into impotent silence.

The church has always reaped what she has sown. The fruit of an insipid, diluted gospel has been the bittersweet experience of a church at peace. When we preached of the love, joy and peace which comes through Jesus Christ we failed to convince the world and simply succeeded in convincing ourselves. Instead of enlisting men and women in the army of the King we have trained them up into an easy-believing indifference which will never threaten the world, the flesh, or the Devil.

All it needed, Satan reasoned, was for the church to lose her vocation of spiritual warfare and turn to the materialistic comforts of peace and he would have won an important battle, if not the war. So it turned out. 'The early church was not an organisation merely, not a movement, but a walking incarnation of spiritual energy. The church began in power, moved in power, and moved just as long as she had power. When she no longer had power she dug in for safety and sought to conserve her gains.'[2] So it remains. The church may have insured her position in a declining, decadent society, but an immobile church is an impotent church – that is an altogether unhealthy

56

place to be! When we mortgaged our spirituality for security we wrote out our own Christian death warrant.

Nowadays, the very idea of the Christian as a man of war is utterly abhorrent to the vast majority of our English congregations. The mere possibility of conflict with society, of being unpopular, or of appearing actually to be different is sufficient to frighten many into a state of something between apostasy and tactful withdrawal. A little boy was sitting in an English church on a Sunday morning. The congregation began to pray. A few seconds later, as he looked at the sea of bowed heads and hand-covered eyes, the boy loudly whispered, 'Mummy, who are we all hiding from?'

Today, it is springtime in the church. The winter of many years is now past and God is again looking for fighters.

Jesus is able to provide the weapons and to guarantee the ultimate victory because he has triumphed already. We do not have to gain the ground; Jesus has already done that. But we do need to hold on to it, to raise the standard of Jesus and there establish his kingship. Men and women are needed who will no longer merely believe the right things but will actively practise them. Fighters are needed who will wear the helmet of salvation, the breastplate of righteousness, the equipment of the gospel of faith, their bodies girded with truth, and who will use the sword of the Spirit to beat the enemy into submission (cf. Eph. 6:10–17). It is worth noting that no armour is provided for our backs because the time for retreat is gone. So many are left with crippled Christian lives simply because they are running away, leaving their backs exposed to the salvos of Satan.

The call to be fighters in the army of the King has implications which have for many years been unacceptable and left undisclosed: 'Share in suffering as a good soldier'. 'No soldier on service gets entangled in civilian pursuits . . . his aim is to satisfy the one who enlisted him' (2 Tim.

2:3–4). The call comes to usher in a new sense of discipline, stability and consistency in our lives; being open to face suffering and hardship for the Lord who faced death for us. The call is to a detachment from the world, not in terms of an isolationist or monastic principle, but 'holiness' (Greek *hagios*), being prepared to be different in lifestyle so that our love for Jesus dominates our lives. Along with this comes a new devotion to the Lord who is over us, and a new determination and desire to please him in all we do. This kind of radical discipleship has always been the call of Jesus, that in our lifestyle we might overcome the three main sources of evil in our universe – the world, the flesh, and the Devil.

It is only when we stand against these in the authority of our God that we will again trouble the evil one by living as soldiers bent on his annihilation. C. T. Studd wrote in his autobiography:

> O let us not rust out – let us not glide through the world and then slip quietly out, without having even blown the trumpets loud and long for our blessed Redeemer. At the very least let us see to it that the Devil holds a thanksgiving service in hell when he gets the news of our departure from the field of battle.

The world

The world (Greek *naos* or *kosmos*) possesses three major connotations:

1. It is a *geographical location*. A place made for the glory of God as the home for his people. Man's rebellion in the Garden of Eden began the process of depravity which has taken that which was 'good' in the sight of God and reduced it to what we are left with today. All things were made by God and were good as created by him, but they were designed to be enjoyed as man lived under the authority of his creator.

Rebellion ruined everything. Sin wrote the bill of divorce between God and man which lasted (with the sole exception of Israel – God's chosen people) until Calvary. In his years of freedom Satan brought man's world right under the control of his demonic activities. God's kingdom of light was transferred to new management and became Satan's playground of darkness: 'The whole world is in the power of the evil one' (1 John 5:19).

Disease, famine, war, disaster and death follow one upon the other. Mankind in his awful ignorance glibly attributes the guilt to a convenient God whose existence is largely denied on all other occasions. Meanwhile Satan, knowing that no one would ever blame him, continues his catastrophic careerings across the planet. Modern man has slowly realised that something has gone wrong with his world, but the remedy he cannot grasp. As Harold Coppin commented, 'Anyone who still feels that this world is in a good state ought to have his TV set examined!'

2. The world is also the name for *an attitude.* The consequences of the fall have been immense but nowhere are they seen more clearly than in the heart-principle of a man or woman. We know we were made to be more than we are but we cannot change and without divine activity initiated by Jesus Christ there is absolutely nothing that we can do. Our world has been totally corrupted and we cannot live with the depression and depravity induced by that thought. To save ourselves we create our own dichotomy pretending that our own part of the world is still healthy and wholesome. We seek to build on, and believe in, a foundation rooted in nothing firmer than fantasy.

That which we regard as the good created from our own efforts we term 'the spiritual' while the rest is 'the secular' or 'the world'.

3. It is the name given to *people outside of the control of Jesus Christ.* The society that we term 'the world' has been

questioning and searching for answers for so long, seeking to come to terms with one question, 'Why?' In a modern-day television parable 'The Prisoner', a computer controlled the inhabitants of a village on an island. The 'Prisoner' challenged and blew up the computer by just asking that one question, 'Why?' In other words, the world is still lost, seeking, yet knowing no answers except live for today, for tomorrow we die. The whole 'live for today' philosophy becomes so real because no one can see tomorrow. There is just no raison d'être for life so all we can do is live.

Andrew Lloyd Webber and Tim Rice summed it all up in the latter's closing lyrics for their first rock opera:

I closed my eyes, drew back the curtain
To see for certain what I thought I knew.
Far, far away, someone was weeping,
But the world was sleeping. Any dream will do.
. . . The colours faded into darkness
I was left alone,
May I return to the beginning,
The light is dimming and the dream is too,
The world and I, we are still waiting,
Still hesitating. Any dream will do.[3]

Only one man has ever provided an adequate solution to the basic problems of the world and man's identity within that world. This solution was so unacceptable that its author was crucified. If Jesus had come offering men the chance to change themselves then he might have been received gladly, but for coming to offer a cross they nailed him to one instead.

The world is so tied to its Prince, Lucifer, that it will always hate Jesus. Meanwhile, the Christian can never be more than his Lord so we can never expect more than hatred and bitter opposition from a world which we are called to live in and to love. That is not to say that we have a right to compromise with the world. We don't. The compromise that stamps out many of the dealings the Christian has within the world represents a futile gesture of peacemaking, a gesture which not only do we have no right to make but which at best can only produce a hollow, empty alliance. We have no right to be at peace with the world. We were made to turn the world upside down but the opposite has occurred – the world has turned the church upside down.

Called to wage war against the world; called to draw men and women with our weapons of love to Jesus; called to stand in authority against the immorality and ungodliness of our society; we have settled for a policy of appeasement and an unholy peace which we had no right to make.

In a radio broadcast about Christian dissidents in the Soviet Union on 9th June, 1977, an Orthodox priest said this:

> We are at the front. In the front line. And this front line is all around us because the enemy has surrounded us on all sides. We are surrounded by the godless. There is not a single place which is free from attack – the press, art, the theatre, schools, official institutions, everything is occupied by the godless. The laws are designed to suffocate religion. We have been at the front for a long time, many of us have been taken prisoner, one might almost say that the whole front has been captured. Anyone who can hear us, respond. Do not believe those who try to dismiss the danger. The aim of the enemy is to destroy us, he has no other aims. But having destroyed us, he will destroy you as well. Listen, listen all those who can hear, we are alive, after all the terrible attacks, after all the awful bombardments, we are *still* alive. But we need help. Help us in every way you can.[4]

In an age when Christian missionaries are murdered in Africa and Christians are imprisoned and oppressed worldwide, we are afflicted by doubt, depression, apathy, confusion and bewildering changes; attacked by the vast spread of spiritism, occultism and modern cults. In this age we must realise that there is a war on. John Stuart Mill concluded, 'War is an ugly thing, but not the ugliest of things: the decayed and degraded state of moral and patriotic feeling which thinks nothing is worth a war is worse.' We need to rise up in love and demonstrate to a dying world that the victory will always belong to our King.

We are in Christ, but he has placed us in the world. We have no right to dismiss that world but only to seek to draw it back to the love of Jesus. This ministry of reconciliation does not require compromise, but holiness; not weakness, but strength to love: not abdication of our responsibilities, nor over-involvement in what the world offers, but a beautiful affection and passion for God. That is something which can express itself practically and demonstrably to the world. One Baptist minister gave this instruction to his son when he was being ordained into the ministry: 'Ted, my son, keep close to God. Ted, my son, keep close to man. Ted, my son, bring God and man together.'

There are two very obvious dangers for each of us who call ourselves 'Christians'.

1. It is very easy to be *too earthly-minded to be any heavenly use*. It is so easy to use our 'concern' for the world as an excuse for going and doing the things that we just want to do. For years it has been the fashion for many Christians to believe that because they don't smoke, drink, gamble or dance they are not 'worldly'. Yet, the spirit of the world can still pervade their whole character. It will show itself in lust, jealousy, over-competitiveness, self-indulgence and many other ways. If you want to serve God in a secular situation you first need to be spiritually ready to do it. An obvious example lies in contemporary Christian music. Many are rightly concerned for quality

and professionalism in presentation, but can easily forget that our lives need to be equally immaculate if we are to be totally used by God. We can never deserve God's blessing, but we need to desire to be used because our lives are being changed by his Spirit. It is so easy in seeking to reach others to ignore the faults in ourselves – and that we must never do. If our lives do not match the words that we say then our lives must change.

While Satan has tried to convince us that by not doing certain things we can claim a standard of holiness, God's way is never merely negative. We are called to be a light to the world and salt to the earth. Salt in the Middle East acted as both a fertiliser and a detergent, a means of encouraging growth and a cleansing agent. That is exactly what we need to be – a positive force for God within our society, honouring him, denouncing evil, and living in his character. Our lives should naturally and spontaneously draw people to Jesus. This should not simply be by reflecting the things that we don't and won't do, but by presenting the very positive and dynamic lifestyle which Jesus sets us at liberty to enjoy. This is seen to be attractive because we have so obviously found someone who has changed our lives. We need to have lost our lives and found them again in Jesus; to have presented them as living sacrifices. This means that we are no longer leading self-denying but legalistic lives in our own strength, but truly liberated ones in his grace and power alone. 'I' must simply become a vehicle through whom God can demonstrate his reality and restore a corrupt and fallen humanity to himself, as he chooses and not as I dictate. In other words, I need to be sold out.

2. The second danger is being *too heavenly-minded to be of any earthly use*. English Christianity has lived under the delusions of nineteenth-century grandeur for too long. We have failed to recognise our own spiritual bankruptcy, failed to notice how out-of-touch we have become with the realities of everyday existence. We have really become

so self-confident and assured as to no longer notice our frightful inadequacies.

Recently an English evangelist was addressing some Christian leaders behind the Iron Curtain. He said, 'Brethren, those of us in Britain want you to know that we are praying for you.' His tone was patronising, but despite the condescension back came the gracious reply, 'But brother we are praying for you.'

They had noticed what we need to see: lack of persecution makes men spiritually flabby, unaware of the crying needs of society, unable to live in the authority of Christ. Unless repentance comes in that situation we die to spiritual power.

Jesus gave us two warnings: 'Let any one who thinks that he stands take heed lest he fall' (1 Cor. 10:12) and 'Take care lest this liberty of yours somehow become a stumbling block to the weak' (1 Cor. 8:9). With those in mind we must live our lives as he did. Jesus loved men, he shared their agony and loneliness, he met them where they were, and told it like it is. Through all his life, his attitudes and his words, he revealed his Father. He went where religious leaders could see only filth, he met the 'worldly', he broke the traditional, and yet he never sunk to the lowest common denominator. Instead Jesus raised men up to where he was and brought them to his Father. No one was too sick or old, too infamous or dirty, for the Lord of glory. What he was in the world is what we *must* be. It will mean that the Spirit of God must teach us to love men and women as Jesus did so that a pure, selfless giving might direct our lives and reach our society, our world, before it is too late. We all have a part to play and a job to do. We must come out of hiding and face up to the world – but only in the power of the King. We were never called to be popular but to be faithful. Jesus said, 'We must work the works of him who sent me, while it is day; night comes, when no one can work' (John 9:4).

The flesh

What is my flesh? Is it just the super-abundance of the flesh that so many of us are frantically trying to get rid of by diet-sheets, etc? Or is it instead a deeper principle summed up years ago in the simple phrase 'I'm doing my own thing'?

'But I want to be me!' This was my first basic expression as a young Christian. Yes, Jesus could direct me and live within me providing he never touched the depths of my life. I would allow Jesus to change me providing I could agree with the planned rearrangements which must also not be too radical. So my early days as a Christian were spent in warfare. No, not fighting to subdue the flesh, but fighting God to preserve my 'self-life'; the 'I' in me, because that is what the flesh really is.

It is not that God wants to come along with a divine sledgehammer and smash us beyond all recognition. No, but he does want slowly to shape and mould us so that we come to resemble Jesus rather than just ourselves. It is the action of a loving Father rather than a tyrranical dictator. What God is doing is remaking us into the original mould to which we were to be cast in pre-creation days. This restoration to the image of God will only begin when we allow God's Spirit to start his work in us.

Some have tried to control the flesh by prayer and regulations, vainly trying to mortify and discipline the flesh by a continuing process of self-examination, striving, defeat, self accusation and self-control.

In the end we realise that flesh is the one thing in the universe that is utterly irredeemable and unchangeable. and only God can change us. Paul wrote, 'Why do you submit to regulations . . . according to human precepts and doctrines? These have indeed an appearance of wisdom in promoting rigor of devotion and self-abasement and severity to the body, but they are of no value in checking the indulgence of the flesh' (Col. 2:20, 22–3). However many times we try and promise to be different, the flesh always seems to reassert itself. In desperation we call to God and back comes the answer, 'You will never change yourselves.' God's way is so simple. We become flesh by being born, we lose it by dying. God does not change flesh, he crucifies it and brings you into life.

The flesh cannot be refined, only crucified!

It is amazing how much of what we do begins well in the Spirit but terminates in the flesh. Only that which comes out of waiting on God, depending on his Spirit, living in his strength is unquestionably not of the flesh. Watchman Nee wrote, 'The old creation is willing to do anything – even submit to God – if only it is allowed to live and be active.'[5] It is not important how good an action may be, the question is what source does it come from? All the flesh wants is to be central, whether that is achieved through sin or good deeds is almost irrelevant. Time and again as a preacher I have seen how the flesh will not lie down: God speaks through a sermon and up springs the flesh, 'Cor, you were good tonight, have to preach that one again. Particularly when so and so's there to hear you!'

This may have scared you. How can we know when we are living in the flesh and when in the spirit? Do we blindly hop from one to the other? Surely forgiveness of sin is sufficient? The answer to the flesh is that it must be fought, we must battle against it. 'Christ delivers the believer completely from the power of sin through the cross that sin may not reign again; but by the Holy Spirit who dwells in the believer, Christ enables him to overcome self daily and obey him perfectly. Liberation from sin is an accomplished fact; denial of self is to be a daily experience.' Jesus does not merely want the works of the flesh destroyed, but the very flesh itself.

Two thousand years after he suffered, Jesus reaches down from the cross to draw us to be crucified with him. To die to our passions, ideals, and our flesh. Paul could

66

say, 'I have been crucified with Christ; it is no longer I who live, but Christ who lives in me' (Gal. 2:20). When that has happened and we are learning, as Paul did, to die daily, then our lives begin to be lost in God. An apple tree does not produce bananas, nor will our lives produce the works of the flesh. If we are rooted and grounded in Jesus, relaxing our lives in his arms, then we are totally safe and victory is ours.

There is a danger when dealing with the flesh of relying too much on isolated incidents or experiences, when what is needed is not a momentary event but an ongoing crucifixion of the flesh and a new deepening of our love for the Lord. We may not notice that much is changing, but it will be and others will see it before we do. One day we will hit a crisis and think that we are bound to fall, but we will not because we are held up by Jesus himself.

When the Russians invaded Czechoslovakia the story is told of a church which was praying. A Russian soldier leapt off a tank and ran into the church. He levelled a sub-machine gun and demanded, 'Anyone not prepared to die for Jesus leave now.' Half the congregation struggled to reach the door but the other half bowed in silent prayer. The soldier challenged them again but no one moved. So he threw his gun to the floor and said, 'Hallelujah, because I'm a Christian too. I just wanted to have fellowship with those who wouldn't betray me!'

When the flesh is being crucified, we'll stand, even in the crisis! It is only by dying to the flesh that we will ever allow the room in our lives for the Spirit to live in. A genuine spiritual renewal must take place in us as individuals in order that daily we might develop that disciplined, consistent, stable Christian lifestyle which will enable us to overcome the flesh.

The devil

To many people today Satan is presented as a most

attractive personality. To a society which doubts that God can be personal Satan presents no such problem. No longer is the Devil seen as a long-horned, spiked-tail Lucifer but as the embodiment of the only supernatural alternative to a materialistic world. In the United States alone CBS News could report that belief in a personal Devil had increased by 11 per cent in only a decade. Our English education system even offers the possibility of specialised courses in witchcraft and the occult.

While interest in a personal God declines among young people in Britain, experimentation with the occult increases alarmingly. One friend of mine dabbled in ouija, seance, levitation, astral projection and the beginnings of ritual magic until he finally met someone who led him to commit his life to Jesus. He was sixteen! Interest in the psychic arts, horoscopes, UFO's, tarot cards, and so on, has reached an unprecedented peak, while young people in the churches of this land see no danger in having their fortunes told.

Satan is on the march, and his aim, as always, remains simple and straightforward. He knows that in no way can he prevent Jesus from returning for his people resplendent with personal glory, so he concentrates his diabolical energies against the church as the people of God. In this way he seeks to nullify the significance of Christ's overwhelming victory. In today's world the attack has been reversed.

The Devil has become a box-office hit and interest in the supernatural has focused on his activities while totally ignoring the church of Christ. Young Christians have proved far from immune to the challenges of their environment, and Satan has not been slow to encourage an unhealthy interest among those who have no need to learn about his more sensational activities. The plethora of commercial literature aimed at this market bears adequate testimony to the potential profitability of the Devil in commercial terms!

C. S. Lewis summarised the argument by declaring,

'There are two equal and opposite errors into which our race can fall about devils. One is to disbelieve their existence. The other is to believe and to feel an excessive and unhealthy interest in them. They themselves are equally pleased by both errors and hail materialist or magician with the same delight.'[6]

Satan is the supreme example of the consequences of rebellion against our almighty God. He begins his existence as a created being, an angel of light, but one whose pride in his own position and character led him to lead the most tragic revolt in the whole pageant of world history. Never was anything more doomed to fail. Despite his failure in the heavenlies Satan determined to try again here on earth. He is on the prowl as the enemy of mankind and we need to know and beware of our enemy. Christians in Britain today need to regain five long-lost positions in regard to our attitude toward the Devil.

1. *Satan is not just an impersonal force for evil*, he is a personal devil. Pope Paul VI was right to insist that 'whoever refuses to acknowledge (a personal devil's) existence is beyond the pale of biblical ecclesiastical teaching.' Satan is revealed time and again in the Scriptures as a personal opponent who rules over vast hordes of similarly fallen angels providing the backbone for his legions of demon spirits. These forces are divided into principalities, powers, the world rulers of this present darkness, the spiritual hosts of wickedness in the heavenly places. He reigns as 'the king of demons'. Not content with being the chief co-ordinator of all created beings, he lusted for the reins of universal government! 'You defiled your holiness with lust for gain' (cf. Ezek. 28:15–19).

Satan stands as an individual, but Satan does not stand alone. When he fell heaven was really deprived of an upright and beautiful angel, Shakespeare commented, 'Angels are bright still, though the brightest fell.'[7] With him fell many of his angelic cohorts 'who abandoned their original rank and left their proper home' (Jude 6, LB

69

footnote) and together they command and co-ordinate an army of demon spirits practising devious tricks and demonstrations of evil.

2. *This world is not a playground but a battleground.* The creation of angels preceded the creation of the earth. When the world was made angels were there to rejoice. Mankind was then made as the pinnacle of creation. Being formed in the image of the King, man was unique as God's creative masterpiece. Jealousy had motivated Satan's rebellion. Envious of God's supremacy the Devil switched his attack from the heavenlies to this earth in an attempt to regain a little of his credibility! Satan has tried to win his battle for planet Earth by gaining control of the hearts and lives of men and women. In this he has gained a measure of success.

3. *Satan is no alternative to the Almighty.* Many evangelical Christians have allowed their own fears and anxieties to so dominate their understanding of evil that Satan has been ascribed to a position far higher than the Scriptures ever give him. In this respect Satan is truly the 'Father of lies'; he has always wanted people to see him as the only viable alternative to the Almighty God.

Satan started out as an angel of light whose personal jealousy led him to aspire to be God. Those heights Satan can never reach. Satan was only a created being. C. S. Lewis wrote of him. 'The commonest question is whether I really "believe in the devil". Now if by "the devil" you mean a power opposite God and, like God, self-existent from all eternity, the answer is certainly No. There is no uncreated being except God. God has no opposite. No being could attain "a perfect badness" opposite to the perfect goodness of God. Satan, the leader or dictator of devils, is the opposite not of God, but of Michael.'[8]

4. *So many see Satan as lonely, and have sympathy for the Devil.* Nothing could be further from the truth. Hidden behind a veil of invisibility hordes of demons are being marshalled into an enormous army the like of which our

universe has never seen. Meanwhile, our nonchalant, casual world, so obsessed with a mindless materialism, calmly ignores all it cannot see with human eyes and the Devil prepares his own Pentecost for the earth. It is the calm before the storm, but no one realises it!

5. *The world and the church have equally to realise in reality that Satan can never win.* Modern day interest in the Devil and his ways is by no means the sole prerogative of non-Christians. Many Christians have talked of 'necessary information', knowing your enemy, as their excuse for paying the normal exorbitant prices to watch *The Exorcist*, *The Omen*, or to read the varying journalistic equivalents of *Witchcraft Today*. For some the reasons may be genuine and the need obvious, but for many Christians excuses are sought to rationalise an orgy of fleshly indulgence which the Lord could never ratify. A genuine enquirer will not merely seek to research Satan from the world but will turn dissatisfied from its glossy de-luxe Devil to the fallen Satan of the inspired Scriptures.

For its part society is now hell-bent on avoiding any value-judgment of Satan, his work, or personality. His very name conjures up all kinds of fascinating chills in the spine. The Devil is a very commercially successful commodity and so a very palatable form of evil decorates our bookstores and cinema screens nationwide.

The church loves losers; we have always had sympathy for the underdog but it's time we stopped exercising a negligent sympathy for the Devil. He rarely bothers troubling us. It is much safer for him to let us get on with our lackadaisical lifestyles and our easy-going indifference towards him. He knows that most of us would rather see our friends and acquaintances drift into hell than raise a murmur of protest that might actually cause them a degree of embarrassment.

Millions of our countrymen are being seduced by the commercial production of ouija-boards, tarot cards, astrology guides and textbooks on magic yet never a word do

71

we raise in protest. 'There shall not be found among you any one who . . . practices divination, a soothsayer, or an augur, or a sorcerer . . . For whoever does these things is an abomination to the Lord' (Deut. 18:10–12). Sex and violence on our TV screens occasionally raise a squeak of indignation within us but the overt selling of Satan and his ways would never induce a sufficient reaction to make us protest to a salesman or boycott a store for retailing such items. Such action need not be spiteful or vindictive, many live in total ignorance and a word of protest given as warning or explanation is often welcomed. At the very least the drift into sin is exposed and our guilt of indifference can be assuaged. Martin Luther King once made the forcible point that when we arrive in glory we shall have to apologise at least as much for the indifference and apathy of the good as for the direct action of the bad. Satan always conquers when good men stay silent. A vacuum cannot long remain unfilled – the question is who will seize hold of the situation and enter in where no angel ever feared to tread.

From the way Satan parades his wares you might be forgiven for swallowing his deceit and thinking that he had been the victor in the eternal conflict instead of its loser.

One sunny day in the late AD 20s Satan looked out on this earth and saw one man living in the power and authority of the Holy Spirit. So he tried three times to turn him. Satan failed. This was without precedent and panic set in so the Devil put that man on a cross and rubbed his hands with glee knowing that with death as the battleground he just could not lose. Three days later the man, who was also almighty God incarnate, broke out of the grave and is still alive today. Before Satan could get his breath back there were 3,000 living in the power of the Spirit, then 30,000, then 300,000 and Satan's been running scared ever since!

Having been utterly and totally defeated once and for all by a crucified man, Satan had to revert to different tactics. As he could no longer win he could only try to convince people that defeat was only a temporary set-back and that his power remained. In that limited aim Satan has enjoyed much success in Britain.

Satan is the 'accuser of the brethren' – the Baptists, Methodists, Anglicans along with everyone else. He is 'the father of lies'. The Christian has no need to be deceived. We gave our lives to the King and he wants to make us into such an army that we will calmly walk over all the deceits of the Devil and into the sunshine of freedom of life in the King of glory.

Satan is called 'the prince of this world'. He has his army. The principalities and powers who rule over nations may be equated with 'the Prince of Persia' who sought to prevent the answer to Daniel's prayers. To this earth as the headquarters of Satan's demonic rebellion Jesus had to come with a cross. Now the victory has been won and it really is time that we started to live in the sublime good of being a victorious people who can hold the ground which our Lord has won for us.

In the charismatic conference at Rome in 1975 God gave this word to his people:

Because I love you,
I want to show you what I am doing in the world today.
I want to prepare you for what is to come.
Days of darkness are coming on the world,
days of tribulation –
buildings that are now standing will not be standing:
supports that are there for my people now will not be there.
I want you to be prepared, my people, to know me, to cleave to me, and to have me in a way deeper than ever before.

I will lead you into the desert –
I will strip you of everything that you are depending upon now, until you depend just on me.

A time of darkness is coming on the world
but a time of glory is coming for my Church.
I will pour out on you all the gifts of my Spirit.
I will prepare you for a spiritual combat.
I will prepare you for a time of evangelism that the
 world has never seen.

I speak to you now on the dawn of my new age for my
 Church.
Prepare yourselves for the action that I begin.
Things that you see around you will change.
The combat that you must enter now is different, and
 you need wisdom from God that you do not yet have.
Open your hearts to prepare yourselves for me, and for
 the days I have not begun.

My Church will be different,
My people will be different.
Difficulties and trials will come upon you.
They will send for you to take your life, but I will sup-
 port you.
Come to me now.
Bend yourselves together now around me.
I am calling you to receive my power.
I am forming a mighty army.
I am renewing my people – I will free the world.

Perhaps the greatest privilege we have is that we live
at this time in history. At such a time as this the fight is
at its most intense for the time for the dominion of the
King draws near. As we recognise the battle, we need to
become the army that will fight as we have been told to
and rise up to demonstrate the victory of Jesus who has
won the battle already.

And you . . . God made alive together with him, having
forgiven us all our trespasses, having cancelled the band
which stood against us with its legal demands; this he
set aside, nailing it to the cross. He disarmed the princi-

palities and powers and made a public example of them, triumphing over them in him. Therefore . . . if with Christ you died to the elemental spirits of the universe, why do you live as if you still belonged to the world? (Col. 2:13–15, 20).

For when the One Great Scorer comes
  To write against your name,
He marks – not that you won or lost –
  But how you played the game.

Grantland Rice

The old college try

This is a wonderful philosophy when it comes to golf, bridge, or football. But it's a lousy attitude in relation to the church. The question here is, 'Did you get the job done or not?' Never mind how hard you tried, how strenuous your effort, how gracious you are in defeat. The church cannot take refuge in nobility and sportsmanship when there are hungry people to feed, sick people to heal, naked people to clothe.

Maybe it's how you played the game that matters to you. But the hungry, the sick, and the naked are looking for a winner.

Wes Seeliger

5:

How can our church grow?

The gospel is a much more powerful weapon for the renewal of society than is our Marxist philosophy, but all the same it is we who will finally beat you. We are only a handful, and you Christians are numbered by the million. But if you remember the story of Gideon and his three hundred companions, you will understand why I'm right.

We communists do not play with words. We are realists, and seeing that we are determined to achieve our objects, we know how to obtain the means. Of our salaries and wages, we only keep what is strictly necessary, and we give up the rest for propaganda purposes. To this propaganda we also 'consecrate' all our free time and part of our holidays.

You however, only give a little time and hardly any money for the spreading of the gospel of Christ. How can anybody believe in the supreme value of this gospel if you do not practise it, if you do not spread it, and if you sacrifice neither time nor money for it?

Believe me, it is we who will win, for we believe in our communist message and we are ready to sacrifice everything – even our lives – in order that social justice shall triumph. But you people are afraid to soil your hands.[1]

Obviously the opposition doesn't view us as being much of a threat!

One accepts that it is always easier to see what is wrong with an institution rather than what is right with it, and yet, there must always be a time when the failures should be exposed and the weaknesses corrected. We stand, right now, in the middle of a spiritual conflagration, the like of which the world has not seen since Lucifer and his angels fell from grace. But we do not even seem to realise that war has been declared.

The problems which would be tolerably acceptable in peace time are no less than catastrophic in a time of war. A quiet indifference covered by the thin veneer of respectable piety marks us out to be spiritual pacifists. Don't you know there's a war on!

In their organisation, their theology, and their ways of relating to the world, our churches today are for the most part merely richer and shinier versions of their nineteenth-century parents. Their organisation (residential parishes) is based on the sociological patterns of about 1885 . . . Their Sunday-at-eleven culture is timed to fall between the two milking hours in the agricultural society. Sermons remain one of the last forms of public discourse where it is culturally forbidden to talk back . . . the church remains a patriarchal, agricultural pre-scientific relic.[2]

For too long this glib jingle has preserved at least an element of truth when applied to the church of Christ in Britain:

> Like a mighty tortoise,
> Moves the church of God,
> Brothers, we are treading
> Where we've always trod.
> Very much divided,
> Not one body we,

Strong on faith and doctrine
Short on charity.

It would be only too easy for us to regard the church as merely the institution, the building or the clergy, but it *is* the people. *The people*, that means you and I, who actively perpetuate the present situation; so in describing the failure of the church to grow in twentieth-century Britain, we are, in fact, describing our failure to bring about that growth.

We have sought to justify our failure at home by pointing to the successes overseas, living in the delusions of an empire that disappeared long ago. Missions are of course vital, and so is missionary concern, but we are always called to begin at home. Leonard Ravenhill summarised it in these words: 'This generation of preachers is responsible for this generation of sinners. At the very doors of our churches are the masses – unwon because they are unreached. Unreached because they are unloved. Thank God for all that is being done for the missions overseas. Yet it is strangely true that we can get more "apparent" concern for people across the world than for our perishing neighbours across the street.'[3]

We must never dismiss our critical faculties, but these should not lead us into a blind destructivism, an attitude of mere criticism. Instead we should draw our conclusions as the outline of a challenge which, together in Christ, we as the church can meet.

A deep sense of spiritual depression seems to pervade the church in Britain. Decline in numbers, lack of clergy and lay-leadership, increasing costs and dilapidated buildings have all combined to induce within us an attitude of near despair at our lack of growth.

In 1976 David Pawson could write, 'We live with the legacy of rising years of decline. Every major denomination in this country has been reporting a decline for sixty years. Roughly since the beginning of World War I.'

The BBC reported (also in 1976) that Sunday school attendance had declined by 70 per cent in five years.

That sense of depression still pervades the church and yet some things have begun to change. We must not neglect what the Lord is doing among us, even at this late hour. Both Anglican and Baptist denominations today point to an increase in church membership! There does seem to be some evidence that the Spirit of God is raising up a radical move among Christians in our land. Some churches have started to grow. Poynton Baptist Church has grown from 5 to 350 members within a decade. In Ashington, the number of Christians has grown from 17 to over 200. St Andrews Church in Chorley Wood have more than 550 members today. Major growth has been seen in the West at St Philip's and St Jacob's, Bristol, in the Midlands at St John's Harborne, in the North at St Michael-le-Belfry, York, along with many more.

On a smaller scale, in one South-Eastern town a new church has grown from 6 members in 1970 to 120 today along with two 'daughter' congregations and combined meetings with hundreds of other Christians in the area.

This is, of course, not a total picture. For many churches the only time that growth is thought of is when a thermometer is erected outside the church to measure financial increase towards the purchase of the new church roof! Many churches have been demolished or turned into furniture warehouses. Far, far worse is the way that many enormous mausoleums serve as the final spiritual home for dwindling, dying congregations.

Clearly, there are some very solid reasons for this failure to grow. By failing to plan we have often planned to fail, leaving the growth of a few churches to demonstrate the potential that still remains today. An over-preoccupation with the status quo and the building (when there is no mention of church buildings in the New Testament) combined with an unwillingness to let go and press forward with God have successfully crippled that great

80

potential. What has not been stifled has been the qualitative difference in the lives of the people of God. A group, often 20 to 30 per cent of the church, have become increasingly vocal in raising three very basic questions of church leadership in this land.

1. Why when much of the church worldwide is seeing growth, and when there are some outstanding examples of the same phenomena in this country, do the vast majority of churches still record either decline or merely the same level of membership or active support?

2. When will traditionalism and man-made structures be sacrificed on the altar of a genuine desire to meet the needs and culture of the late twentieth century?

3. When will we mobilise our forces, instead of remaining inactive? When will we be prepared to launch out with a strategy designed under the guidance of the Holy Spirit for both quantitative and qualitative growth?

An answer to any of these questions could occupy a whole book. Each requires the same necessary prerequisite which lies in the area of our unity and commitment to one another as the people of God. This alone explains the tremendous biblical emphasis on the corporate identity of the people of God. We need to recognise that the keystone to powerful Christian living lies in our really being one with each other.

We need to attempt answers to these three questions. But first we have to recognise that, while we cannot totally explain our failure to expand either spiritually or numerically by any one factor, a major contribution to our problem has come from our attitude to the body of Christ.

Church on the move

In the New Testament everyone was scattered around and about with the exception of most of the apostles. Throughout the first century the church was the missionary society and her members were the missionaries. They were the 'sent-out' people who gossiped the gospel throughout the then-known civilised world. Today, the opposite applies. The missionaries go out while the church stays at home. It will only be when we rediscover what it is to mobilise every church member into active Christian service that our world will ever be turned upside down.

When the Christian message is communicated through the lives and words of every Christian in the market-place of their own secular situation, then the gospel will always be at its most effective. 'Behave wisely towards those outside your own number; use the present opportunity to the full. Let your conversation be always gracious, and never insipid; study how best to talk with each person you meet' (Col. 4:5–6 NEB). Dr Max Warren commented, 'The analogy of the market place remains true to life. I well remember attending a service of Holy Communion in a remote part of Nigeria. It was a great gathering of over six hundred communicants. After the service, I asked how the gospel had reached this area, and I was told that it was due to two market women who gossiped to such good effect that many became curious and asked for someone to teach them about this "new way". To a far greater extent than is commonly realised Africa has been evangelised by gossiping the gospel.'[4]

The New Testament church, as portrayed in Acts, provides a very vivid illustration of this principle.

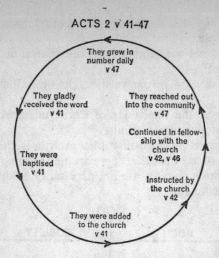

This circular process went on repeating itself until the writer of the Acts of the Apostles can record 'the church throughout all Judea and Galilee and Samaria had peace and was built up; and walking in the fear of the Lord and in the comfort of the Holy Spirit it was multiplied' (9:31).

Thus we can clearly see that the early church were not satisfied with proclaiming the gospel, or even with making converts. Their aim was always to obey the Lord's command to make disciples. The evangelistic goal was not fulfilled until new converts became responsible, reproducing Christians and part of responsible, reproducing congregations. We need to understand that the church is not only God's agent of evangelism but she must also be the goal of true biblical evangelism. Jesus said, 'I will build my church; and the gates of hell shall not prevail against it' (Matt. 16:18).

'Is it enough even to say the ultimate goal of evangelism is to make disciples? *The goal of evangelism is the formation of the Christian community.* It is making disciples and, further forming these disciples into living cells of

83

the body of Christ – new expressions of the community of God's people.'[5]

We will not see growth from the church of Christ in Britain until:—

1. We develop in our relationship with God and one another.

2. We see the total body of Christ mobilised into an active reproducing community.

3. We start to recognise that growth is the natural corollary of spiritual life. If we are not growing upwards and outwards then we are not necessarily dead, it is just likely that we are!

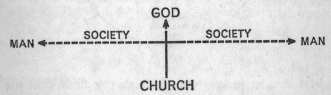

The traditions of the elders

It really is strange that in most churches we cannot identify where biblical injunction ends and church traditions begin! We can so easily claim that what we do is biblical when it is nothing more than traditional. In so many churches the slightest challenge to the established order is regarded as a serious threat and not given a moment's scrutiny – a scrutiny which the New Testament enjoins. In the same way any challenge to live our lives from a different perspective is equally feared.

Recently I took a girl with me to sing at a major evangelical church in London; her ministry was tremendously well accepted. However, she wore trousers, not to be controversial, she just didn't know it would be offensive. The pastor laughed with me afterwards that no one else had ever done that! The next week I received a letter of complaint, very graciously written, but asking that we fall in line with the Scripture. I still can't find the reference –

perhaps it is 'Thou shalt not wear trousers in church to sing from the platform' (Hezek. 14:5)!

We do need to understand why traditions in our churches and in our own lives are so important to us. Why are we so slow to allow substantive changes to take place in our own lives and in the life of the church as a whole? We can find many reasons, yet perhaps four stand out as demanding comment.

1. *Insecurity*. We live in a society riddled with insecurity. Will my marriage survive? My children rebel? Will there be petrol for my car? Will I become redundant? Will my world, itself, survive? This insecurity comes right into our Christian lives as something of a neurotic hangover. We spend time knotted up inside, frequently feeling troubled and threatened constantly needing to see tangible evidence of either love and commitment or of continuing long-established structures and realities. One might say that the material age has undercut the very essence of the spiritual dimension in mankind. We become so dreadfully fearful of change, particularly if it challenges our authority and/or leadership.

Imagine the reactions of your church leadership, or yourself, when faced with these suggestions for your church.

(a) The church must remove her inward-orientated programmes (i.e. indrag) and adopt outward orientated forms suitable to our society (i.e. outreach).

(b) The church must recognise her role to 'hate evil and love good, and establish justice' (Amos 5:15) by seeking to develop community help projects in her area.

(c) The church must give her members time to develop relationships and minister to other individuals outside the formal agencies of the church.

(d) The church should divide her membership into teams or groups for both formal and informal Bible study, witness and prayer.

(e) The church must seek to adapt her forms of worship

in preparation for the twenty-first century.

These would only be moderate suggestions for change in our churches. Judging by the furore aroused by suggesting we change our times of meeting or service orders, these suggestions would reduce many of us to positive apoplexy. If only we earthed our security in God, instead of in our man-made structures. Our problems may date from childhood relationships with parents, with mistreatment at school, teenage rejection, or many other difficulties. Fine, then we should turn to God for healing. We have no right to allow our problems to shackle the people of God. The pioneering, changing church needs to be released from the chains we put on her – stop worrying, our God reigns. He's taken care of the past and he'll lead us into a glorious future as well.

2. *Future shock*. In our pasts we have all suffered rejection and hurt. To trust an unseen God for an unseen future is a massive trauma for today's Western materialist. To launch out blindly into following Jesus has to be branded as fanaticism because we dread the consequences of leaving our nets, our foundations, as the disciples did. If God tells us in advance what lies in store, that really helps; if not then the unknown appals us!

What we need is a regular and radical reappraisal of faith along with its continual exercise if we are not to fall foul of obesity and therefore immobility. God wants us to trust him for the future. Some years ago I went to Newcastle-on-Tyne for a fortnight's mission all over the city. Unfortunately I did not keep in touch with Ruth, my wife, by telephone but by letter. No letter reached her for some time and I could not be contacted by telephone, so she had no address at which to contact me. We had only been married a few months and had still to work out our communications systems! What I had not realised when I left home was that she only had ten pence in her purse and her bank account was overdrawn! With no means of contacting me, having to go to college each day, with almost no food in the larder, Ruth wondered what to do. She decided that as we both 'lived by faith', through the commitment and support of God's people, she would tell nobody about her plight. We had so often seen God provide, so Ruth thought she would pray and see what happened.

For nine days no money came! The tenth day a cheque for thirty pounds arrived. Every day in between something happened which we had never seen before. Food would arrive on the doorstep. Someone would arrive with transport to college; an invitation for a meal; milk, eggs, and cheese – and no one knew her predicament. When I arrived home I was greeted with the same ten pence. 'Look at the birds of the air: they neither sow nor reap nor gather into barns, and yet your heavenly Father feeds them. Are you not of more value than they? . . . Therefore do not be anxious about tomorrow' (Matt. 6:26, 34). The God who looks after today is perfectly able to care for tomorrow as well.

3. *Individuality*. Man is not an island. However, twentieth century man likes to think he is. It is one of his favourite delusions. It is worth recording that one of the major signs of wealth in our society is a detached house. Detachment and apparent independence are seen as prizes to be valued.

We find it far more difficult to live in the corporate than in the individual. We find it far easier being personal failures. We bitterly resent the idea of being vulnerable in relationship with others. We look at all the occasions when others have failed us, have let us down even when we trusted them. Out of our disillusionment comes our mistrust of the way our Lord designed us – not to live as individuals but as a corporate body in him, mutually interdependent, one on another.

4. *Rigidity*. A real sense of inflexibility rules our attitude towards change. The very idea of God as a creative Lord constantly doing new things, moving us on, adapting and changing us to be more like him, is always subordinated to the idea of Jesus as 'the same, yesterday, today and for-

ever'. Our natural conservatism shows out in so many ways. The church has, for so long, stood as the defender and preserver of the status quo and the Church of England was long ago labelled 'The Tory Party on its knees'.

This dislike of change has prohibited us from joining in with much that God would do among us. The word came to Isaiah. 'I am the Lord, your holy one, the creator of Israel, your King . . . Remember not the former things, nor consider the things of old. Behold I am doing a new thing' (Isa. 43:15, 18–19). We tend to forget that Jesus turned water into wine and walked on water. He always has been an enterprising and exciting leader. The traditions of the Temple gained little sympathy from him. The story of how he cleansed the Temple of its non-biblical accretions was considered sufficiently important to be included not just in one gospel but in all four!

When we face adventure set against stability, the unknown or the well tried, the uncertain or the secure, our common sense will always tell us to take the latter. It takes a deep, inner determination to change, to go on, to discover the dynamic life-changing love of God.

Religious history shows two phases, the dynamic and the static.

The dynamic periods were those heroic times when God's people stirred themselves to do the Lord's bidding and went out fearlessly to carry his witness to the world. They exchanged the safety of inaction for the hazards of God-inspired progress. Invariably the power of God followed such action. The miracles of God went when and where his people went; it stayed when his people stopped.

The static periods were those times when the people of God tired of the struggle and sought a life of peace and security. Then they busied themselves trying to conserve the gains made in those more daring times when the power of God moved among them.[6]

For too long the sense of daring, of God-sanctified courage and imagination has been lost in the church. Far too often things have been sanctified in our church practice by the traditions of the elders rather than the will of a God who will not be fossilised by inactivity or bound up by our institutions.

We have a God who is marching on. It is time we followed. The four problems just outlined have provided all the necessary ingredients for a bitter recipe of disaster. The result has been a weak, fearful, insipid body totally unprepared and unable to launch out in God. We are too afraid to trust God to supply our needs and lead us out into the unknown. The world fails to see in Christ's alternative society anything which would inspire confidence and satisfy man's longing to see something of excitement and adventure, yet also of eternal value. Bill McSweeney of York University wrote in *The Times* of 16th, April 1977: 'Not many years ago, a plausible case could still be made for the survival of the Christian churches. But things have got worse . . . Who wants to belong to a church that has nothing to offer but a secular version of the gospels, that has lost the nerve to evangelise and takes refuge in the smug alleluias of pentecostalism.'

Our position is paralleled by that of the children of Israel during their wilderness period. We have escaped from Egypt in that we have turned from our old lifestyle which we lived directly for ourselves, but have failed to come into the Promised Land of a life lived totally to God. What is more, we besiege the throne of the King who brought us out of the past with all our longing and complaint for what we've left behind. The punishment that God always gives for failing to press on, to believe that he is worth following will be an aimless wandering in the wilderness. That is not what we were made for. A few months could have taken Israel into the Promised Land – instead she wasted forty years. God always looks for a people who will risk their comfort and security in order to

Z

pioneer his way. Instead we nestle back into the safety of the established respectability of our own conventions and traditions. We need, again, to hear the prophetic, discerning words of Charles Finney: 'An overconcern with forms, ceremonies and non-essentials gives evidence of a backslidden heart!'

When will my church grow?

No individual answer will ever be totally adequate. In subsequent chapters we will look at relationships and spiritual maturity, but in this chapter we must face the question and look at the implications of growth.

VISION

| RELATIONSHIPS | MATURITY | GROWTH |
| among the membership | of the membership | from the membership |

But with all the talk of church growth, strategy, goals, etc, we must not ignore the priorities of relationships and maturity. Let it be clearly stated at the outset, a church will not grow without right relationships providing a church for someone to be converted into; nor will it grow without prayer and the correctly developing spiritual lives of the members. If those two prerequisites are met, then (and only then) can a church grow on a firm foundation.

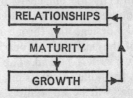

RELATIONSHIPS
↓
MATURITY
↓
GROWTH

In diagnosing the problems to growth within the British church, Eddie Gibbs who heads up the Bible Society's Department of Church Growth, has come up with thirteen diseases which afflict the church:

Maintenance complex – just keeping the thing going!

Failure syndrome – we tried it all before, and it won't work here.

Credibility gap – the gap between what we say we are, and what we show ourselves to be.

Overcrowding – full churches can also be a problem, though a rare one!

Ecumania – postponing mission in the interests of getting together with other churches.

Ethnicitis – middle-class evangelism which expects other cultures, classes or nationalities to come to us on our terms.

People blindness – failure to recognise that some people are different to us!

Old age – when everything else has gone but a resident group is left which is so busy dealing with the problems of the past that they can't adapt to new situations.

Leadership tensions – management problems caused by growth meeting inexperienced leadership which is unable to cope.

Fellowshipitis – including home groups that are a protest against all that is relevant.

Structure strain – nineteenth-century structures that will not change.

Nominality – how do you bring second-generation Christians into a first-generation experience?

Remnantitis – those who see their situation as Custer's last stand!

These represent a major cross-section of the problems in our churches which prevent growth! But 'is growth essential?' you may ask. The Scriptures certainly do not seem to deny the validity of tracing numerical growth – indeed Luke carefully recorded the growth pattern of the Jerusalem church:

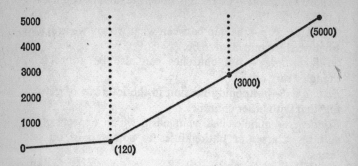

ACTS 1 v 15   ACTS 2 v 41–42   ACTS 4 v 4

5000

4000

3000 (3000)

2000

1000

0 ———— (120)

(5000)

From there the congregation was multiplied into multitudes, from then on the multiplication was seen not in a congregation but in numbers of churches.

Numerical expansion must never be regarded as the alternative for spiritual maturity and growth among the church membership. Growth must be both qualitative and quantitative.

'If the Spirit of God is moving the church it must be growing God-wards in obedience and outwards into the world, winning more and more people into its membership . . . If a relatively small number of people are feeding well on a good diet of Word and Sacrament, then there is a danger of middle-aged spread.'[7]

Take this suggested conversation between a church leader and Eddie Gibbs:

'So why aren't we growing?'

'Well I've just given thirteen reasons that could apply.'

'Yes, but only ten of them apply. So why aren't we growing?'

'Get rid of the ten reasons and we find out.'

Basically when God anointed us to be his life-giving body in our society we received all that we need. If we aren't growing and developing in the healthy way that we should – then remove the obstruction to growth!

The objection comes back, 'I can't change my church. Do I leave?'

By no means. Each of us has the opportunity to demonstrate what can happen by our individual activity. Why do we always wait for everyone else to join us. If we do something – a church could change.

Try talking to one or two friends, keep your minister and/or elders in touch and try something:

(a) Street work
(b) A coffee bar
(c) Church youth group
(d) Neighbourhood fellowship group
(e) Coffee morning
(f) Young wives group
(g) Supper club
(h) Visitation

Anything, in fact, which gives you the opportunity of meeting people where they are, and not just where you want them to be. Pray hard first so that God guides you to what he has for you. Make sure that what you're attempting is going to communicate to people. So often like attracts like and there's nothing wrong with trying to reach people of your age, nationality and culture.

Set yourself goals, make plans, start finding others who can help and get the whole church joining in prayer. Try getting one of the national evangelistic agencies to give help and advice if not actual training for the task – then get on with it. Seek to reach the unchurched and in communicating Jesus draw them into the family of God as well. Make sure you don't just allow things to go on for ever. Set a time limit and then evaluate in the light of what was initially attempted (i.e. look back over your earlier goals) – then consult with the church.

This very brief summary needs some underlining:–

1. *Your relationship with the church.* In spite of all the frustration you didn't leave! You stuck it out and asked

for support. If that support was denied for this project and any other then you might have had grounds to consider leaving. No, you involved the church. Who knows, if God blessed the effort the whole church might start (and it needs to) asking questions you asked. At the very best you might not only have brought a few to Jesus but started to remotivate a church.

2. *You didn't try to do it alone!* Right from the start you involved others whose gifts and talents will, almost inevitably, be different to yours. That way they would act as the necessary check on you and together you would learn from each other.

3. *You set goals and time limits.* The aim was evangelistic. All these aspects of the project could provide some measurable indication of success. The project could therefore provide evidence to challenge the whole church to evangelism.

4. *It was not just another meeting added to the church calendar and conducted by professionals.* Nor was it just aimed at those on the fringe of the churches – the results would affect us in all our relationships with non-Christians from then on. Often the results of such an effort will be seen more in our own lives, prompted and encouraged by the teaching and training we receive, than anywhere else.

5. *It produced prayer and concern in the church.* It turned eyes outwards to catch sight of the world outside and prompted a new involvement within society.

If the project was just allowed to drift along, unchecked for years, then it would also, in turn, become institutionalised. Instead, when it has wound up many other ideas will probably spin off from it. You may well find that you have started a snowball rolling down a hill, small at the top but very different by the time it reaches the bottom.

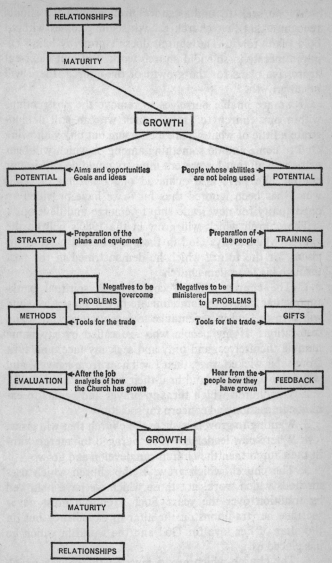

RELATIONSHIPS

MATURITY

GROWTH

POTENTIAL ←Aims and opportunities
Goals and ideas

People whose abilities→
are not being used

POTENTIAL

STRATEGY ←Preparation of the
plans and equipment

Preparation of→
the people

TRAINING

Negatives to be
overcome

PROBLEMS

Negatives to be
ministered to

PROBLEMS

METHODS ←Tools for the trade

Tools for the trade→

GIFTS

EVALUATION ←After the job
analysis of how
the Church has grown

Hear from the→
people how they
have grown

FEEDBACK

GROWTH

MATURITY

RELATIONSHIPS

'As we seek to understand church growth we should recognise that . . . church growth seldom comes without bold plans for it. The church doesn't grow by being engaged merely in splendid church work. Without clear-cut aggressive plans for the growth of the church, there will be no growth.'[8]

If we are unable ourselves to remove the obstructions within our church to growth, then we can still demonstrate a little of what we are all missing out on by allowing God to come and do something among us which will bear witness to all that his present ministry could do within our church. We have also achieved one other major point which has been ignored thus far – we have provided an opportunity for new leadership to emerge and develop.

The church which will grow in the 1980's will be the church which obeys God in these areas, and catches his vision for the future which he demonstrated in the past through his Jerusalem church.

1. The church which recognises her spiritual bankruptcy, her failure to communicate to her generation, and will turn to God in repentance to receive forgiveness and restoration. 'If my people who are called by my name humble themselves, and pray and seek my face, and turn from their wicked ways, then I will hear from heaven, and will forgive their sin and heal their land' (2 Chron. 7:14).

2. The church which turns to prayer and begins to exhibit compassion and concern for society.

3. Wanting to grow is basic to the church that will grow.

4. Where new leadership is encouraged to emerge within the church then the church can develop and grow.

5. The church which grows is the church which uses methods which work, not those which we have hallowed by tradition over the years. Such a church must never sacrifice her traditions on the altar of expediency but on the altar of her love for God and the world in which he has placed us.

6. The church which grows must be the church which

seeks to teach, train and mobilise its entire membership into active Christian service.

7. Unless we set both long-term and short-term goals we will only be able to use church membership as the barometer of our growth. As our growth must be wider than that, we should set out now how we feel God would have us change and grow. No goals, and for too long, no growth. Goals smash our comfortable maintenance of the status quo and point us to where we could be going.

There are only two options open to the church today: one is to struggle to patch up the contemporary church, retaining all we can of traditional forms and patterns of life, resisting with all our might the forces that demand change (until the whole edifice crumbles as a new generation rejecting empty form, and seeing no meaning, abandons our churches – leaving them to die as gracefully as possible). The other option is to accept the challenge of change and to channel it – to seek to build together a church which will be a true expression of the church, yet uniquely suited to our twenty-first-century world.[9]

The latter is the challenge which we must face. We change or we die – evangelism has always been about change (in the lives of individuals). Today it must face the supreme challenge – *change in the church*.

Commitment to one another

Let us open up ourselves to one another,
Without fear of being hurt or turned away,
For we need to confess our weaknesses
To be covered by our brothers love,
To be real
And learn our true identity.

For we are all part of one another,
We cannot hope to live life fully on our own.
We each possess a precious part of our father's nature,
And together we'll become that perfect whole.

And God shall surely build his living temple,
Of people set completely free; loving and appreciating one
another,
Enjoying life in its entirety.

Many shall be drawn to us and wonder,
At the peace and the love and the joy that shall never die,
They will drink from that stream of living water,
Flowing out from the fulness of our lives.

So help us to understand each other,
In a new and living way,
Not just accepting words that are spoken in themselves

But by speaking more freely
And listening more clearly
We shall understand the spirit that is within.

Let us open up ourselves to one another,
Without fear of being hurt or turned away,
For we need to confess our weaknesses
To be covered by our brothers love,
To be real
And learn our true identity.

Dave Bilborough

6:
Footwashing for beginners

It has always been easy to theorise about Christianity, to diagnose collective answers to the malaise which afflicts the British church today. There is a certain comfort in coming up with theological solutions to problems which we always set in an abstract and impersonal context. The further the problems can be removed from ourselves the safer we feel.

I will never forget preaching one evening on the subject of unity and then finding at the end a young married woman crying her eyes out. I went up to her, adopting my best pastoral manner (such as it is), and putting my arm around her asked what the trouble was. 'I don't know how to say this – but I just don't like you,' she replied. It's fine talking about a subject in the abstract, but I was shattered to gain a crash course in first hand experience! It was all I could do to keep my arm around her and pray that God who is the author of love would create it where none existed. From that day to this I have been grateful to that person for her honesty which made me consider how to live the truths we so glibly preach.

Jesus ordained that the way the world would really know who he is would not be by the propagation of right doctrine, or by the performance of correct ritual, but by the way in which Christians love one another. Our unity was to be the classic demonstration of the way Jesus is united with his Father: it would be the vindication to the world of his incredible position as son of God and of the glorious status of the church as Jesus' body on earth and his bride-to-be in heaven.

'The glory which thou hast given me I have given to them, that they may be one even as we are one, I in them and thou in me, that they may become perfectly one, so that the world may know that thou hast sent me and hast loved them even as thou hast loved me' (John 17:22–3).

To a world which continually demands a miracle, or at least a sign, Jesus left the greatest wonder of all. Not simply a healing, a feeding of 5,000, the subjection of a storm to his will, or even a resurrection. Instead he prayed to his Father no less than four times in John 17 that old and young, rich and poor, upper classes and lower classes – his church – might be one. In other words that the church of Christ might be the one place in society where there was no racial discrimination, class-preference, generation gap or any other form of division. This was to be the greatest miracle of all. A society of all different kinds of people, yet bonded together in loving commitment as one body, because they loved Jesus.

Today's world is still looking for that new alternative society. In a survey commissioned by Cuthbert Bardsley (then Bishop of Coventry) non-Christians were asked what changes they would most like to see in the lives of Christians. The reply was threefold: a more casual attitude to material possessions, a new sense of gaiety, and a greater togetherness.

Even that is not so new: just 150 years after the death of Jesus the church historian Tertullian recorded that the pagans accused Christians of many things. They accused them of cannibalism, they misunderstood the communion service to be a drunken orgy, and yet Tertullian says that there was one thing which the pagans could not ignore: they kept saying in amazement to each other, 'See how these Christians love one another.'

For too long we have told young converts that when they became Christians Jesus comes to live in their lives to bring forgiveness for their sin and to introduce his new lifestyle. We have forgotten to add that they also became part of a whole new family. God only recognises brothers and sisters joined together in his family. We might find each other difficult, we might not have chosen one another, but we are lumbered with each other and it is time we learned to work together and love each other in a way which truly reflects our obedience to and faith in the commandments of our Lord.

If Christianity were simply a religion to which mental assent alone was required, then there would be room within it for those with cold, unfeeling hearts. It is not. Essentially Christianity can never be reduced to an unfeeling, academic theology. Christianity is not about a doctrine but about a person. The question can never be 'What do we know about him?' (i.e. head) but must be 'What does he mean to us? (i.e. heart). Because Christianity is a relationship with God rather than merely a religion about him it must transcend the level of words alone. Our love for one another has similarly to go beyond a mere lip-service to the principles of unity, and unity must be an experienced and observable part of our church life.

How often do people gaze in wonder at our love for one another?

How often do we really put the feelings and needs of others above ourselves?

How concerned are we for each other?

How much encouragement and visible love and commitment do we really give each other?

What about those 'we just do not like'?

If we fail to love our fellow Christians, how can we claim to show God's glory to the world? That glory is not just revealed through an individual, but through the corporate identity of a people who belong to Jesus. The two expressions are inseparable. The people of God must in

102

their relationships together reveal the glory of the living God to the world in which they live. 'By this all men will know that you are my disciples, if you have love for one another.'

For our part we need to recognise at once that we are never going to convince people by intellectual argument alone. For so long people have been *told* the gospel We have threatened, cajoled, argued, preached, laid on special services, concerts, baptisms and films. Hundreds of thousands of words have been uttered, tens of thousands of pounds spent, and yet our land remains stubbornly pagan. We need to recognise that words have never been enough. The kingdom of God is among us. It is time to show people the reality we have only told them about. 'Words, words, words – I am sick of words. Sing me no song, read me no rhyme, don't waste my time – show me.'[1]

We must accept that we have concentrated our energies on being individuals when our Lord has been looking for a community. This in no way reduces our individual personalities, rather it fulfils them. What we can never find alone we can experience together. That is why loving one another is so foundational. Without that loving commitment we fail to function to a fraction of our full potential. As S. D. Gordon said, 'Co-operation increases efficiency in amazing proportions. Two working together in perfect agreement have fivefold the efficiency of the same two working separately.'

God has given us one another in order that together we might complement each other. He has not made us all the same, like a bunch of evangelical Homepride flour graders rolling off a conveyor belt. It was never his purpose that we should only share with those who are like we are, but that together we should balance each other.

So often we attempt to live out our Christian lives while being cut off from the rest of the body. Imagine the horrible noises which result when your hand changes gear in a car without your foot pressing on the clutch. All too often we try to be bigtoes running up the road doing our own thing instead of living and moving in unity with our brothers and sisters. As Paul wrote, 'If the whole body consists of eyes, how does it hear?' (1 Cor. 12:17). In the same way each of us has different functions to carry out in the body of Christ. None of us is meant to try to be God's answer to everything and everybody. We were not made that way. We were made to live and work together to God's glory – we may not all be equal, but we are all one.

That is why the independence which we so overtly practise grieves the heart of God. If we think of a project, a mission, an event, we so often fail to ask who else is doing this. We do not ask because we do not want to know. We would rather run something ourselves and have our own little independent work than join in with anyone else who might then have authority over us. That is why we have so many missions doing a particular work with no thought of how our co-operation would promote the kingdom. We compete and we duplicate because we will not sacrifice our independence.

I have often heard preachers ask the condemnatory question, 'Where will you be if Jesus comes tomorrow?' I suspect that he won't come tomorrow. He prayed that his people might be one and that prayer of Jesus is still on the slate. We are not one because we love ourselves too much. We would never dream of going to 'the other' Christian coffee-bar in town to say can we join with you? We would never do that if we could still proudly go it alone, confusing the world and dividing the people of God. Jesus can't come tomorrow because he is coming for a bride, but if he came tomorrow what would he find?

Picture the bridegroom on his wedding day. The organ plays softly while he waits for his bride to appear. The best man nudges him and he glances lovingly over his shoulder – to be greeted by an arm bounding up the aisle, closely followed by two or three toes, a fingernail, an elbow joint or two, the torso, and then a head all rolling alone. If Jesus came today that is what he would find. Not a beautiful bride, ready dressed and waiting, but either bits and pieces or a wrinkled old hag, bent with age, crippled with arthritis, and dressed in a shabby, torn wedding dress. What a bride for the Lord of glory!

When you stubbornly follow your own self-glorifying, selfish will you decimate the bride of Christ and your punishment awaits. Our credibility in heaven will not depend on the results we obtained on earth but on the way we have treated each other and the humble submission we have given to one another. Jeff Schiffmayer, one of the clergy at The Church of The Redeemer in Houston, Texas, put it like this. 'The first lesson we had to learn as a body is still the most important one: the effectiveness of our ministry depends upon the fervency of our love for each other.'

The commands of Scripture are far too clear to be either ignored or misunderstood: 'A new commandment I give to you, that you love one another' (John 13:34). 'He who says he is in the light and hates his brother is in the darkness still' (1 John 2:9). 'Whoever does not do right is not of God, nor he who does not love his brother. For this is the message which you have heard from the beginning, that we should love one another' (1 John 3:10–11). 'Beloved if God so loved us, we also ought to love one another' (1 John 4:11).

One of the most significant things about the life of Jesus was that he never just made suggestions but always gave the first demonstration of how to put them into practise. 'When he had washed their feet . . . he said to them . . . If I then, your Lord and teacher, have washed your feet, you also ought to wash one another's feet. For I have given you an example, that you also should do as I have done to you' (John 13:12, 14–15).

We need to learn again what it really means to be committed to one another. In the old Testament, when Ruth became fully committed to Naomi, the Christ comes forth; David and Jonathan become one soul; in Acts we read that believers were one soul – they had learned a real depth of commitment to one another, and out of this unity the power of the Holy Spirit was released. To experience this unity we too have to sacrifice a precious thing – our individuality.

As we learn to lay down in the Spirit that which we treasure most (our own way of doing things, our independence and individuality), we gain a far more precious thing. God comes and reveals his glory in the body. It has always been the purpose of almighty God that his message to mankind might not simply be revealed in words but through the lives of a people who live the message they preach; who live in mutual interdependence and love; who will freely lay their lives open to one another that God might work his own communal miracle by his Spirit. It is never something we can manufacture; but it *is* something which when we desire God will bring through the ministry of his Spirit in the lives of each other.

Through the years of our quest for Christian unity I come more and more to share with many others the conviction that the secret of the unity of the church is the renewal of the church. It is mistaken to say 'unite and renewal will come'; the truth is 'let yourselves be renewed by the Holy Spirit and unity will follow'. This was in essence the teaching of Pope John XXIII and the lesson of Vatican II. It is as churches and Christians yield themselves to the Holy Spirit that in a new nearness to Christ they became nearer to one another.[2]

Some years ago, at the end of a couple of years ministry as a 'solo' evangelist, I received very clear guidance to begin to work with a full-time team of people. Now a team is not a church, but it encapsulates many of the pressures and problems of church relationships into a very short space of time. My first experience of the team occurred on 10th July, 1973. That was the day the team started. It was also the day that I, as its leader, was broken open by God through others on the team. It was an interesting beginning! The three years we spent together are a time I will never forget, or cease to thank God for. Many of the lessons of this chapter were first learned in experience on the team, as together ten people tried to learn how to share Jesus with others. This was only to discover that it was out of our relationship with one another that God really chose to speak a message from our lives and and our relationships, not just from our words.

When you are thrown together with nine, rising to fourteen, other people you do get problems! We had to learn to appreciate the differences in each other, to draw out the talents of each other, to love one another under pressure, to be honest, committed and sincere in all that we did, to relax together, to work together. Instead of being able to hide behind our words we had to go into local churches and live the message we had been given. We were all fairly immature and made far too many mistakes, but God has never been too concerned about the quality of his people when he is only beginning to work within them. By the end, we were not 'super Christians' but we had learned a little of Jesus, and most of that had been gained from each other.

Graham Kendrick was part of that team and he perhaps gave the best summary of the time we all spent together. 'Becoming part of a team ministry has been a priceless experience. It has often proved painful too, but then the love of Christ came not without pain for it led him to the cross. Taking his example we have had to begin to learn how to share ourselves, to love one another, to walk "in the light" together, that in the words of Jesus, "By this will all men know that you are my disciples, if you have love one for another." '

Many of the lessons which we needed to learn as a team need to be relearned by the church, and then worked

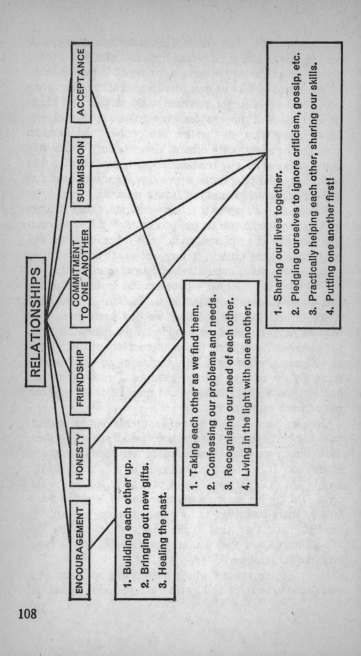

RELATIONSHIPS

ENCOURAGEMENT
HONESTY
FRIENDSHIP
COMMITMENT TO ONE ANOTHER
SUBMISSION
ACCEPTANCE

1. Building each other up.
2. Bringing out new gifts.
3. Healing the past.

1. Taking each other as we find them.
2. Confessing our problems and needs.
3. Recognising our need of each other.
4. Living in the light with one another.

1. Sharing our lives together.
2. Pledging ourselves to ignore criticism, gossip, etc.
3. Practically helping each other, sharing our skills.
4. Putting one another first!

108

out in our daily lifestyles and relationships. We need to put one another first in concrete, practical terms, so that we are no longer ruled by our own selfish desires.

One of the first steps towards this is to start being really honest with one another. It is time we lost the inhibitions we seem to have genealogically ingrained in us as Englishmen, and really started to share ourselves with one another. One of the most tragic faults which exists within the church of Christ in this country lies in the fact that we can go to church Sunday by Sunday, year by year, and never really get to know and love those we worship alongside. For too long our churches have been little more than preaching centres or activity generators, and the observable beauty of the real relationship of the community of God has been sadly lacking.

Sunday by Sunday thousands leave our churches for the minister/elder/pastor to shake hands at the door and ask 'How are you?' and back comes the all embracing reply 'Fine.' Despite the way which we truly feel we always try to keep the intelligent enquirer at arm's length. Sometimes it is because we would rather keep our problems, more often it is because we are scared to share ourselves. One could reconstruct that Sunday morning conversation adding the thoughts behind the words in brackets.

'How are you?'
'I'm fine' (I feel lousy really – but then!).
'How's the wife?'
'She's fine' (why on earth I married that woman I just can't imagine).
'How are the children?'
'They're fine' (they are also the reason the wife's in such a state, scream, scream, scream, especially the little one).
'And how's your job?'
'Fine' (you stupid . . . don't you know half the firm were made redundant last week, and I'm one of them).

'And how's your spiritual life?'

'Fine' (well with that lot going on what on earth do you think it's like!).

Such dishonesty is not confined to congregations. A few years ago a young married couple I knew were asked how they were at the door of their south coast Baptist church. When they then said, 'It's really dreadful, we just don't know what to do,' all the minister came back with was, 'Fine, good evening,' because he could not cope either.

Behind the extremes we are all a little bit like that. We hide behind a plastic grin, smiling to cover the deep hurt which we feel inside. If only we would open ourselves to one another and realise that God never intended us to struggle along as 'loners' but to live joyfully as the community of faith. Most people who come to me with problems of bitterness, resentment, bad relationships with their brothers and sisters have gained those problems because of the total absence of real communication. If we could expose ourselves to one another, share the real person inside us, and receive the love and counsel of deep friendship in return, then so much would be different. If only we could allow ourselves to be vulnerable to one another, to share the deep things, and if the Christian community could then really minister to our real problems and hurts, how different things would be.

Whatever our problems may be, whether economic, racial, psychological, sexual or anything else we should know that there is a supporting community in the churches of Britain. That, however, presupposes that we have first learned to be honest and open ourselves. 'But if we walk in the light, as he is in the light, we have fellowship with one another, and the blood of Jesus his son cleanses us from all sin' (1 John 1:7).

Walking in the light together; being utterly open with one another; sharing our lives together in honesty, is a startling experience. To find that people love us for what

110

we are, knowing what we are, and in spite of what we are, instead of loving us because they see the counterfeit spirituality which we have so carefully nurtured for their benefit, that is a tremendously liberating fact.

When we have removed the sham, we find we are free to be what we are and not what we would like to be. Then the people of God can meet me where I am and together we can journey, aiding each other, to that position in God which we want to attain.

There are, however, two tremendous problems in all this; first, how do we get clear of the problems of the past and second, what if when we are open and honest people condemn us instead of lovingly caring for us and accepting us as we are?

So many of us have long standing problems with our fellow Christians, that it is good to recognise where the problems lie.

1. It is no good taking the attitude that we just don't get on with someone and using that as a justification for having problems with them. Of course, it is quite true that God made us all so different in character that we won't automatically get on with everybody. But Jesus commands us to love one another, and he does not tell us to do something without giving us the strength to carry it out. Some relationships will be harder to form than others, some will just fall into place, and others will take months of working out. It is often the relationships which have to be worked at, between those of opposite character, that prove to be the deepest and most profitable. We cannot excuse ourselves by saying we just don't get on. If you both want to, and open yourselves to God's direction – you will! As has often been observed: 'If you have got problems with people – you got problems.'

2. We always find it easier to get on with those we agree with, but not those of a different doctrinal or denominational viewpoint. It is not necessary for us to agree together on *every* jot and tittle of doctrine. Some things are,

of course, non negotiable; but in general terms our agreement together does not come from uniformity of theology. Indeed, most Christians would barely know what the word means! Agreement is not based on law and doctrine but on our mutual love for Jesus and commitment to his will. As John Noble has so aptly put it, 'Father forgive us our denominations as we forgive those who denomination against us.'

3. We must never isolate a particular incident and use it to justify our breaking off relations with our brother or sister. Mutual tolerance seems to be missing so very often between us. This is particularly true when someone hurts us. So often we cannot see that particular instance as anything but a deliberate attack on us, and yet if we share it with the person concerned they would be horrified. So often when called in to mediate between two Christians I have found the root of the problem to be a total misunderstanding, a throwaway comment, or what was intended to be a harmless joke. Now we need to be careful so that we never intentionally cause our brother to stumble, yet we also need to be aware that everyone has an 'off-day', and everyone makes a mistake.

Even if someone deliberately hurts us we have no right to rise up in righteous indignation cutting ourselves off from them for ever. Have we not often prayed 'Father . . . forgive us the wrong we have done, as we have forgiven those who have wronged us'? Those prayers have been heard, as we have asked God to forgive us in exactly the same way as we forgive others, so he will do. 'For if you forgive others the wrongs they have done, your heavenly Father will also forgive you; but if you do not forgive others, then the wrongs you have done will not be forgiven by your Father' (Matt. 6:13–15, NEB).

4. 'But,' you may say, 'I'm right'! In one way that is pretty irrelevant. The cold harsh voice of orthodoxy has never particularly blessed anyone. Even if we are right we put ourselves in the wrong by our own feelings of pride

and injustice, our 'rightness' is measured not by our academic correctness but by our right attitude of love, sympathy, empathy and support. We have no God-given prerogative to put everybody right, only our loving commitment to somebody can earn us that privilege. As A. W. Tozer once put it, 'Always it is more important that we retain a right spirit towards others, than that we bring them to our way of thinking, even if our way is right.'[3]

We must realise that all problems have two sources, not one. Once we see this, we can go in honesty to one another and confess our own weakness, insecurities and faults. Perhaps by 'speaking the truth in love' we will lose a problem and gain a friend. However, speaking the truth is all very well, but it must always be *'in love'*. Remember that we are dealing with individuals who are delicate and precious in the sight of God, and we are called upon to 'forebear one another in love' (Eph. 4:2).

It is no good going to someone and ungraciously retorting, 'Look I want to put you right. You hurt me the other day. What you did was stupid and you ought to know that.' That's not 'in love'. Remember Paul's words – 'Love is patient and kind; love is not jealous or boastful; it is not arrogant or rude' (1 Cor. 13:3, 4). Love says 'I'm sorry, I misunderstood you the other night. It's made me all bitter or resentful – look could we pray together.' The confession should always be followed by prayer that God will put right what we have allowed to go wrong. By taking the responsibility ourselves we avoid doing to someone else that which has been done to us (i.e. inflicting hurt and condemnation), and we give the relationship a real opportunity for restoration and progress.

This sharing together is not just a good suggestion it is what Jesus commanded – 'If you are offering your gift at the altar, and there remember that your brother has something against you, leave your gift there before the altar and go, first be reconciled to your brother, and then come and offer your gift' (Matt. 5:23–4).

We may, perhaps, have two questions. First, What happens if the person stalks off in a huff because they cannot receive my apology? Well, it may be that they have a bigger problem than you had and you must pray for that person and perhaps share the need with an older Christian from the other person's fellowship. But you have discharged your responsibility and under God you can live in freedom.

The second question is, What do we do if after confession and prayer our bitterness and resentment remains? The first thing is to query our motivation – do we want to be free from bitterness and resentment? Or do we, in fact, rather enjoy having our own problems and indulging in thoughts that we can never change? If our desire for forgiveness and reconciliation is sincere then God both can and will heal our bitterness and resentment. Therefore sometimes we find that we need to go and pray with someone in pastoral authority over us before that freedom is complete. There are various reasons for this but the most obvious is that when we share our needs with others the problems often assume a true sense of proportion, and praying with someone else can give the assurance which we often fail to achieve alone.

Further, even if the problems remain, when we love those who despise us we are obeying Jesus' instructions and therefore we receive the blessing and approval of our King. In nine cases out of ten that I have personally witnessed the conclusion has not been a continuing problem, but a simple 'Why didn't we get together before?' The answer, too often, is that it was because we were too proud and independent to make the first move.

There is a tremendous liberation in learning to walk in the light together. When we discover that people love us as the people we are and not as the plastic blown-up replica of what we would like them to think us to be, then we are really released to be ourselves and build solid relationships with others within the atmosphere of mutual appreciation and commitment. Our weaknesses, anxieties and insecurities can be exposed, prayed through, and dealt with by God as he works through his people. In this way God can restore us to be whole people – and all because we just started off being honest!

In Acts and the epistles we begin to see the church as she really can be. She emerges as a practising community, realising that fellowship was no mere attendance of meetings together but a mutual friendship which extended to all aspects of life and lifestyle. In Acts we read that the church had all things in common. From that foundation, prayer and ministry could come together so that fellowship would really be 'worshipping friendship'.

We need to rediscover these realities today for we belong to a great family which should never just get together for meetings. Jesus died to give us abundance of life, not just abundance of meetings – and so much of our time has become meeting-oriented when the call of Jesus was not just to share our meetings but to share our lives. This sharing should transcend all difficulties of race, colour, class and culture. The church in Antioch discovered what that meant. A black man (Simeon called Niger), an ex-Sanhedrin member (Saul of Tarsus), a Cypriot (Barnabas), King Herod's foster brother (Manaean), and presumably the usual sprinkling of slaves all met together. Jews and Gentiles found a unity in Jesus which overcame all the anti-Semitism and anti-Gentilism of the centuries because they became one in Christ Jesus. Cultural, political and social barriers collapsed. 'The man at the very peak of the social pile and the man at the bottom met together in the church of the Lord Jesus Christ and they were one in a beauty of human relationships.' So comments Francis Schaeffer and concludes, 'Men should see in the church a bold alternative to the way modern men treat people as animals and machines today. There should be something so different that they will listen, something so different it will commend the gospel to them.'[4]

115

While racialism and prejudice still pervade our churches, while preferential treatment is still given to the wealthy and influential, while brothers and sisters walk in blissful ignorance of each other's needs, while these situations are allowed to continue how dare we call ourselves the church of Christ?

I believe with all my heart that if we in England are to avoid being equated with today's Laodicean church, then we must relearn the principles of love and commitment to one another. It has been said so often that the Jerusalem experiment (Acts 2:44; 4:32) in the early church was a failure. That is utter unmitigated rubbish largely formulated as an excuse to avoid facing up to the challenge and demands active pursuit of the original model would entail. We need to recall that from those beginnings the church turned the world completely upside down, and while intricate theology can attempt to destroy Scripture with the myths of dispensationalism ('these things were only for those days'), humble Christianity bows the knee to Jesus and re-establishes the love and friendship which he commands for his people in their practical, everyday relationships.

Practically this means if your brother has insufficient and you have more than you really need – try sharing it. This may sound obvious but what about the money building up in your bank account when your sister is short? What about the car in your garage when a brother needs transport? What about the individual who is lonely because no one ever invites them to come round? What about the spare bed when someone needs somewhere to stay? Threatened or challenged this is where it all begins.

I will never forget being part of a mission team working for a fortnight in a church on the outskirts of Wolverhampton. I stayed with a young married couple, both graduates, who were teachers in a local school. Some months later we met a second time for a couple of hours, and then a third time when the following story emerged.

This couple were very gifted – the husband was an excellent linguist. They had tried to begin a family and settle but had been unsuccessful. Very quietly the Lord had spoken to them and they both felt it right to go to theological college and then on to the mission field in West Africa as Bible translators with the Wycliffe Society. This would mean leaving their home, furniture and wedding presents behind. These had been offered to both sets of parents who had declined the offer, so they had asked God what should be done.

At the time my wife and I had been married for a year and I was just completing my second year as a full-time evangelist. Soon we were to be homeless, but in the past the Lord had provided: ten days before the wedding day we had nowhere to live (my first year as a full-time evangelist had produced £119.00 to live on, plus my parents keeping me alive along with a few other personal gifts), but the Lord provided in his own inimitable style. Right at the last minute, and above all that we could ask or think, we were given half-a-house rent free in London – for a year! What is more it was given by a non-Christian whom we had never met in our lives!

Imagine for a moment, as that year came to an end, hearing this young couple whom we had met for fifteen days offering us their house, furniture and wedding presents which they could not take with them. Their action almost blew the minds of local Christians. Six years later I am still recovering myself! To give, and love and demonstrate it in that way is the most astonishing demonstration of fellowship that I have ever seen. The story is not quite over – their little boy was born a year ago and God has greatly blessed them. I believe we still have to see what God does for those who take him at his word and love and give all that they (literally) have at his simple word of command.

It's time we grasped the reality that fellowship is not just a principle, it's a way of life. It's not just a meeting on

Sundays, but getting to know one another as people. It is a really active sharing; sharing our material needs, our problems, our anxieties, our fears and our blessings – but without embarrassment. 'Little children let us love not merely in theory or in speech, but in deed and in truth – in practice and sincerity' (1 John 3:18).

Finally, let us take this subject out of our peer group and place it in the context of authority and submission. 'I don't really get on with my minister/elders/Crusader class leader/ pastor/youth leader,' is an attitude that could perhaps be best summed up as 'I think I'm allergic to authority! Certainly in this freedom loving age we tend to rebel against authority rather than submitting to it. Biblical phrases like 'you that are younger be subject to the elders. Clothe yourselves, all of you, with humility toward one another' (1 Pet. 5:5) and 'to the humble God shows favour' (Prov. 3:34) are very unpopular. We are so concerned with self-achievement and self-fulfilment that to 'obey your leaders and submit to them' (Heb. 13:17) seems like a needless curtailing of basic human freedoms.

Submission and authority may not be very popular words in this generation but the principles are very clearly laid down in the Bible. In the healing of the centurion's servant he did not say that he was a man *in* authority and because of that he had to be obeyed. Instead, he did say that because he was *under* authority he spoke not with his own authority but with that of Imperial Caesar. The private might be very afraid of the centurion but he certainly respected the whole weight of the Roman Empire.

Similarly, we may not respect our minister, youth leader or anyone else in spiritual authority over us, but they do not speak with their own ideas, they speak with the authority of God. It is the Lord's voice which should be heard, and we must learn to submit to the authority which he gives to them. We may not always agree with what they say – we have a perfect right to share that with them (lovingly!). But if our leaders still insist then we ought to be obedient, even if we still believe that viewpoint to be wrong. For too long disagreement has automatically resulted in division but if leadership is in submission to the church as a whole then we fulfil our obligation before God by being obedient. If the action is wrong then the fault lies with the leaders who will have to face their Lord.

If this makes you think that leadership is something to be desired then try reading Ezekiel 34 or listen to the words of James – 'Let not many of you become teachers, my brethren, for you know that we who teach shall be judged with greater strictness' (3:1). Those in spiritual authority have an incredible responsibility before the Lord and are liable to the judgment of God should they fail. By being submissive we are therefore provided with spiritual covering or protection. Everyone from ministers downward, should be submitted to men of authority who can correct and guide them. Of course, this concept can be elevated out of all proportion and we should beware of those who decide that *they* possess spiritual authority. But we all need to be subject to one another, for none of us has a monopoly on divine truth.

In line with the responsibilities of those over us we also have a tremendous responsibility towards them. For too long the minister/youth leader/elder has had virtually to 'go it alone'. Let's take the example of the average youth leader: in his early twenties, married, young children and a very demanding daytime job. Our responsibility must lie in whole-hearted support, not just in prayer but also in more material ways. It is likely that most of his spare time is devoted to churchwork, meetings, arranging events, counselling, helping and supporting the young people. Very often, the result of this is that he and his wife begin to lose their flair, drive and sparkle. The young people's fellowship will then get dry, criticism and gossip begin, and the group starts to break up.

Instead of this happening we should get together to

consider what is going on. All too often the youth leader and his wife are too burdened with caring for others to care for themselves, and far too few people are actively caring for them. So many of our Christian leaders are made to do far too much, as a result their work and relationships suffer. Too many broken homes and broken marriages among Christian leaders in this country bear ample testimony to this. Too much potential leadership has been lost because people are not prepared to risk their relationships, families and homes. If we were all helping and supporting one another much of this could never happen.

Hence our responsibility is not just to leadership but to all our brothers and sisters. How the world would notice if it saw Christian love and fellowship being exhibited in practical ways.

Who does the shopping, spends an hour sitting and talking, does the gardening, or gets the coal for the elderly folk in the church? Who decorates the young marrieds' house? Who always has time to give practical help? We have so many practical gifts and talents which we could be giving to one another. If only we stopped being 'islands' and functioned as a body it would make such a difference! One day perhaps the accountant will do the mechanic's accounts for him while the mechanic mends the accountant's car. The contact brings fellowship, both jobs are done free of charge and the world loses $33\frac{1}{3}$ per cent!

I am amazed at all that some local Christians do for my wife and I, particularly when I'm away from home. Calling in to make sure Ruth's all right, mending the fence, repairing the record player, baby-sitting, inviting the family out for the day, putting some money through the letter-box each week, making a blackboard for my little girl. If only all of us would get involved, without being asked, in actively loving and caring for one another.

How much of your time is spent demonstrating your love and affection for your brothers and sisters? We can't

120

divide it into secular and spiritual. Whether what we have to offer is comfort and counsel or practical skills we should be doing all we can for one another and thus demonstrating the gospel in action.

> Now if we are called upon to love our neighbour as ourselves when he is not a Christian, how much more – ten thousand times ten thousand times more – should there be beauty in the relationships between true Bible-believing Christians, something so beautiful that the world would be brought up short.[5]

It really is time for us to go up to those to whom we have never talked in the church and quietly commit ourselves to one another.

It is time to go to those against whom we harbour resentment, bitterness or past problems, to confess and get right with one another.

It is time that we demonstrated community in practical terms.

It is time we stopped thinking it spiritual to give for missions but not to my brother who needs shoes.

It is time we learned to appreciate and support one another.

It is time we become the bride of the King who said, 'How good it is and how pleasant for brothers to live together . . . It is like the dew of Hermon falling upon the hills of Zion. There the Lord bestows his blessing, life for evermore' (Psalm 133:1, 3, NEB).

The Holy Spirit

Remember not the former things,
  nor consider the things of old.
Behold, I am doing a new thing;
  now it springs forth, do you not
    perceive it?
I will make a way in the wilderness
  and rivers in the desert . . .
to give drink to my chosen people,
  the people whom I formed for myself
that they might declare my praise.

Isaiah 43:18–21

7:
Power from on high

Once, the world was turned upside down by 120 people filled with the Spirit of God. They were 120 very ordinary people, yet neither their lack of culture, education, background or influence, nor even the power of the mighty Roman Empire, could deflect them from their purpose. 'How could such a very ordinary and somewhat nervous band of 120 disciples, huddled together in prayer in that upper room, launch such a devastating spiritual revolution that the fiercest persecution could not stamp it out?'[1]

That question is being asked throughout our land today. It is the critical question of the radical new generation within the church. We may try to escape giving a reply because the issues that it raises threaten both our security and the status quo, but it is a question that must be answered if we are to avoid a twentieth-century ecclesiastical civil war. Over one hundred years ago Charles Finney gave his classic answer which remains so true today: 'Power from on high is the supreme need of today.'

Western church leaders of the arrogant, self-confident twentieth century have proudly proclaimed, 'The early church had the benefits of ministering in a less-complicated society; it's different now. That can't all happen today.' How wrong can one be?

Never in the whole history of the church has there been a move of God on the scale and magnitude that we

123

are witnessing today. Statistics and viewpoints may differ but over the last few years within parts of Latin America and South-East Asia people have been committing their lives to Jesus Christ at three, or even four times the birth-rate.

In the past revivals have been confined to a limited geographical location, to a brief period of time; yet today mighty moves of God, like the Ruanda revival, have gone on for years and nearly half the civilised world is beginning to experience the power of God at work within society.

Let us take the practical example of the African continent south of the Sudan. In 1900 7 per cent of the population was Christian, by 1978 that figure had grown to over 30 per cent, and if things continue as they have done by the year 2000 no less than 50 per cent of the population will be committed Christians! As Bishop Festo Kivengere has so aptly put it, 'When God moves in *his* time, you can't stop him. Nothing can. This is the East African revival. Story after story, one here, one there – catching a vision and sharing it with others. It's wonderful when God is moving.' That is the statement of revival, from a Ugandan Bishop who has seen his friends die and his family suffer, yet who knows that it is only the Devil's backlash because God is working. Just as genuine moves of the Spirit of God in revival power are being seen world-wide, so we are also seeing the inevitable corollary of our Christian brothers and sisters facing imprisonment, torture and death as the church once faced from the Roman Empire.

What is the reason for all this? Many church leaders have drawn our attention to the words of Joel: 'And in the last days it shall be, God declares, that I will pour out my Spirit upon all flesh' (2:28–32). The argument goes that we are living in the last of the last days. Over the Christian centuries God has chosen, at various times, to move within society in a mighty way – what could be more inevitable than our loving God making one last move for the hearts and lives of men and women. Dr Billy Graham has pointed out nine signs of Christ's second coming; all are being fulfilled today, including one he specifically emphasises – the return of the Jews to their homeland. He quotes Dr Wilbur Smith: 'If you ever wake up some morning and find the Israeli armies have occupied Old Jerusalem, you can know that the end is near.' In June 1967 that is exactly what happened.

It is perhaps not, therefore, too surprising that worldwide the church of Christ should be seeing all the things happening that she is seeing today. New emphases on personal holiness, social concern, evangelism, relationships, all bound up in the person and work of the Holy Spirit, are springing up in the church worldwide. There is a new concern for growth both numerically and in godliness. As D. M. Panton wrote some years ago:

> Vastly more was wrapped up in the descent of the Holy Spirit than the church has yet experienced, or than the world has yet seen; and the Spirit himself thus reveals that while the Christian centuries are 'the last days', and Pentecost began the wonder, we today, standing in the last of the last, are on the edge of a second and more tremendous upheaval of the Holy Spirit . . . so in linking up ourselves with myriads of Christians throughout the globe, in praying for world-revival, world-evangelism and the world-return of our blessed Lord, we are praying for solid coming facts, and therefore, know that we are praying according to the will of God; we are praying for that in which we may have sudden and glorious part; and we are praying for the world the biggest blessing it will ever have on this side of the great throne.[2]

Why then are we not seeing the sovereign movement of the Spirit of God in evangelism and renewal in our country? For so long we have held on to the notion that 'this is a day of small things', but with so much happening elsewhere the church of Christ in Western Europe is having to ask 'Could anything be wrong with us?' One could take that question a little further:

1. Could we be guilty of cheapening and reducing the gospel until it reaches our level? (See chapter 1)
2. Could we be so lacking in compassion that we have failed to care for our neighbours, body, soul and spirit?
3. Could we be too conscious of our social position and too afraid to become 'fools for Christ's sake'? (See chapter 4)
4. Could it be that we lack urgency in prayer?
5. Do we glibly take the credit for that work which belongs to the Spirit of God alone? Watchman Nee has commented, 'If such boasting erupts upon winning only ten souls to the Lord, what will happen should a thousand souls be saved?' In taking glory to ourselves we prevent the living God from giving us that blessing which is the desire of his heart.

All of these represent more than adequate reasons for the reluctance of the holy, righteous God to pour out revival upon our country. We must, however, add one more vital reason – the tremendous suspicion which exists in our land over the person and work of the Holy Spirit. That, above every other reason, could be why we see so little in this country of 'power from on high'.

The Scriptures have much to say about the person and work of the Holy Spirit.

1. He is, first of all, *the promise of Jesus to his people:* 'But, when the Counsellor comes, whom I shall send to you' (John 15:26). He is sent to be the 'Counsellor' (RSV), 'Comforter' (AV); 'Advocate' (NEB) or 'Helper' (NASB). It's always confusing when we have four different translations of one word! In fact, the Holy Spirit is not sent to us to be any one of these things – he is sent to be a counsellor to guide us, a comforter to bless us, a helper to be with us and an advocate to speak on our behalf. All four rolled up in one.

2. He is *the power of God in each one of our lives*. If Jesus himself needed to be anointed with the Holy Spirit (Matt. 3:16) how much more do we. As F. B. Meyer so rightly reminds us, 'Never forget that our Lord's ministry was not in the power of the second person of the blessed Trinity, but in the power of the third person.'

3. He was the one who led Jesus into the wilderness, and is *the one who should guide us today*. Please note that the Holy Spirit is never referred to as a vague impersonal force, an amorphous 'it' but always as 'he', a real, vivid personality living within us to guide and lead us and to reveal Jesus within us. 'He will teach you all things . . . He will bear witness to me' (John 14:26;15:26). Wherever one person of the Trinity goes so will the other two and when the Spirit comes to our lives he brings the Father and the son as well.

4. The Holy Spirit is *the one who evangelises people through us*. We do not have to become devastating 'super Christians' but we must simply allow the Holy Spirit to mobilise and lead us into reaching others. We are reminded that it is 'not by might, nor by power, but by my Spirit, says the Lord' (Zech. 12:1), and it is the Holy Spirit who convicts men and women of the realities of 'sin and of righteousness and of judgment'.

We often picture the Holy Spirit described in John 14 as the 'Comforter' as a kindly, grandfatherly figure trying to mop away our tears and hearts. We forget that the phrase was that of 1611 English and word-meanings change. An alternative rendering is given by the Bayeux Tapestry depicting King William's victory at the Battle of Hastings. One of the sections depicts a reluctant hero being prodded with a spear so that he will actually go and fight. Underneath the caption reads – 'King William comforteth his soldiers'! In exactly the same way the Holy Spirit has been given not just to reassure us but to mobilise us into battle. That is why Jesus told his disciples to go and take the message of his love to their world, but to wait, first of all, for the anointing of his Holy Spirit.

The popular notion that the first obligation of the church is to spread the gospel to the uttermost parts of the earth is false. *Her first obligation is to be spiritually worthy to spread it.* Our Lord said, 'Go ye' but he also said, 'Tarry ye', and the tarrying had to come before the going. Had the disciples gone forth as missionaries before the day of Pentecost it would have been an overwhelming spiritual disaster, for they could have done no more than make converts after their own likeness.[8]

We, as the children of God, having given our lives to the risen Jesus are called to experience the life of this indwelling Spirit within us. Before Jesus died, he warned his disciples that he would have to leave them in order to go to his Father. However, when he then promised to send them his Holy Spirit Jesus came out with this astounding statement: 'Nevertheless, I tell you the truth: it is to your advantage that I go away, for if I do not go away, the Counsellor will not come to you; but if I go, I will send him to you' (John 16:7). In other words, rather than us longing to have 'walked with Jesus by blue Galilee' (an aspiration which seems to possess so many), Jesus has called us to rejoice that he has gone because his departure heralded the arrival of his precious Holy Spirit.

If Jesus was still walking this earth in his physical form we might see him once in our lifetime. We would be able to hear him preach, to see him heal and do miracles, but we would have to live for the rest of our lives on the meaning of it. Instead of Jesus walking across our path once or twice in seventy years, and then only alongside us, we have his Spirit actually living in us every moment of the day. From the very instant that we surrender our lives to Jesus' control the Spirit comes to make his home within us. 'Repent, and be baptised every one of you in the name of Jesus Christ for the forgiveness of your sins; *and you shall* receive the gift of the Holy Spirit' (Acts 2:38).

Why, then, do we find that the mere mention of the name of the Holy Spirit is sufficient in certain circles to put our fellow Christians on to the defensive. Nowadays many of us run in the opposite direction at the mere mention of his name. Division, bitterness, resentment, fears and misunderstandings abound. Our over-reaction has lead in some cases to a new Trinity of 'Father, Son and Holy Scripture'! We are left with only one conclusion: an enemy has done this.

> Satan has opposed the doctrine of the Spirit-filled life about as bitterly as any other doctrine there is. He has confused it, opposed it, surrounded it with false notions and fears. He has blocked every effort of the church of Christ to receive from the Father her divine and blood-bought patrimony. The church has tragically neglected this great liberating truth – that there is now for the child of God a full and wonderful and completely satisfying anointing with the Holy Ghost.
>
> The Spirit-filled life is not a special, de luxe edition of Christianity. It is part and parcel of the total plan of God for his people. There is nothing about the Holy Spirit queer or strange or eerie.[4]

The controversy has centred upon the so-called 'charismatic movement' and claims of 'baptism in the Holy Spirit' along with all kinds of side-effects and side-issues. Perhaps the easiest way to proceed would be to look at the major objections and counter-arguments, in brief, before going further.

1. It has been claimed that in seeking a deeper awareness of the Holy Spirit in the life of the believer we run the danger of falling into fanaticism. I sometimes wonder what our modern-day churches would make of first-century Christians who sold what they possessed, supported each other, shared both their worship and their lives while

communicating the living Christ to their godless society. Would we have branded the apostles as fanatics? For men to live by 'the law of the Spirit of life in Christ Jesus' rather than by 'the law of sin and death' automatically implies that they expected their lives and lifestyles to be different from the rest of society. Is that fanaticism?

It has been said far, far too often, 'Be careful, you can take these things too far.' The Holy Spirit was given to bear witness to Jesus. In so far as we are seeking for him to fill our lives in order that we can become more Christ-like, it is impossible, if not blasphemous, to use words like fanaticism. I heard a lovely definition of a Christian fanatic the other day: 'A Christian fanatic is someone who loves Jesus more than I do.' How very true that comment is! When we see someone whose life is being so transformed by the Spirit of Christ that it makes us feel inferior or embarrassed – we write them off. How dare we?

2. The dangers of over-emotionalism and irrationalism in this case have been mentioned by many. It has certainly been true that in a number of instances Christians have blamed the Holy Spirit for their lack of self-control!
The Holy Spirit can scarcely be accused of our own excesses, be they either those of over-emotionalism or the equal defect of under-emotionalism. It is never the Holy Spirit's fault when we choose to go on an emotional trip! When he created us God gave us emotions, and these we must not ignore. For a long time we have prided ourselves on being British! We have considered our coolness and reserve as symptomatic of our maturity while more emotional races, for example the Latin temperaments, are regarded as being more juvenile. There is no biblical endorsement for our suppressing our emotions. We are proud of not crying, laughing, hugging, sharing and demonstrating how we feel, but this is by no means necessarily a good thing. In fact, we have often been branded 'God's icebergs because we seem to be so afraid of expressing

ourselves in any way other than verbally. Our emotional reaction to individual situations probably owes far more to our own temperaments than anything else. For so long the world has seen Christians proclaiming with gloomy faces 'I'm so happy. Ever since Jesus came into my life it's been really wonderful.' We look more as if we were preparing for a funeral than for a wedding. I will never forget meeting one man leaving a church on a Sunday evening where I had been preaching. He was determined not to shake hands with me so I stood in the doorway so that he had to. With the glummest face I've ever seen he said, 'I've got the joy of the Lord, it's just deep, deep down.' Sometimes I think that if our faces betray our feelings accurately then it would take a couple of North Sea oil derricks to get it up again!

Although we must be careful to avoid the superficial, it will never be any good going through life with a 'Smile Jesus Loves You' on the end of our noses. We must never be satisfied with facial expressions which give the lie to our words. If Jesus really does bring joy we should live that joy out to others. Jesus unsparingly condemned hypocritical sobriety, so must we. It is not virtuous to look miserable. Under-emotionalism can be as wrong as over-emotionalism, but it is nowhere near as unsparingly condemned in most of our churches today.

God is again showing us how to enjoy our Christianity – for many of us this means that we need to be released to live in the freedom that Christ gives to those who love him and are prepared to enjoy his life and lifestyle. Our emotions are subject to our wills, as we relax in the presence of God new freedoms are discovered. The danger is, of course, that we may abuse our liberty and find it disintegrating into the licence of *over*-emotionalism; but the Spirit God gives us is one of 'wisdom, love and self-control'. While our lives are being emptied of self and filled with the Holy Spirit he will certainly introduce us to the joys of being released from pent-up emotions and feelings suppressed for years – but he will never make you what you are not prepared to become.

3. Then, we meet the once and for all argument. It is argued that just as Jesus won his complete victory over Satan in a once and for all encounter on a cross; so we receive all that we need from Jesus in an encounter of commitment which provides for all our lifetime all that we need from the hand of God.

There is, of course, an element of truth in this argument, as indeed there is in each objection outlined here. It is certainly true that when we surrender our whole lives into the hands of Jesus and ask for his forgiveness and indwelling, he hears our prayer, brings his cleansing, and comes to live in us through the person of the Holy Spirit. In that sense the work is finished but in another sense it is far from completed. A marriage can be contracted instantaneously by signing the wedding certificate but it may well take a lifetime to work that marriage through to its fulfilment. I often suggest when preaching that if the married men present loved their wives as they did on their wedding day then their marriages were on the rocks! This is not to infer that love was not present on the wedding day, it probably was quite self-evident. That is not the point – it's only when married that we get behind the pretty, submissive, shapely character we married and start discovering the real person. It is as we discover who our partner really is, and as we get to know them better, that we find love grows and grows and grows.

That is precisely what should be happening in our relationship with Jesus. The saddest words I hear from young Christians are "I wish I loved Jesus as much as when I first met him'. How tragic, when love between people can grow, love with the Lord of glory diminishes with the passage of time. Herein lies one of the major problems of modern-day evangelicalism. We have preached instant conversion, instant forgiveness, instant solution, instant change and forgotten (however true they may be) that Christianity is not all instant. Our relationship with Jesus does not arrive at full maturity in a moment. We have the privilege of using our lifetime to discover more and more of him.

John Stott has put it like this, 'I have been saved, I am being saved and I am going to be saved,' while Paul points to the work of the Holy Spirit as progressive life-changing, 'And we all . . . are being changed into his likeness from one degree of glory to another; for this comes from the Lord who is the Spirit' (2 Cor. 3:18).

We have not arrived with God, we have only started on the pathway. It is only as our lives are day by day emptied of ourselves and filled with the Holy Spirit that we will discover that Jesus is changing us in so many ways that there is an observable difference. St Bernard of Clairveaux said, 'What a man loves he will grow to resemble.' It is only as day by day he draws us to love him more that we will grow to be like Jesus.

4. It has often been argued that the early church saw things happen which we seldom or never see. The signs and wonders, miracles and healings, spontaneous sharing of the gospel, men and women whose faces shone with the joy of Jesus, tongues of fire, speaking with tongues, prophecy – these it is argued, were given for simple people in less-complex days. They are not for now.

This doctrine of dispensationalism suggests that these activities of the Holy Spirit were something specifically for the early church and finished with the death of the apostle John. The argument goes that as the canon of Scripture was being developed such signs and wonders became increasingly irrelevant. It is significant to note that nowhere is this even suggested in the Scriptures, indeed the opposite is clearly stated. It is not that we need either the Holy Spirit or the Scriptures, rather we need both.

The Spirit is bound to the word . . . A church which abandons the link with the Word and tries to rely only on the Spirit falls a prey to all the evils of spiritualistic enthusiasm. Conversely a church which tries to rely on the Word and tries to reduce the Spirit to the Word, falls prey to all the evils of verbalistic enthusiasm.[5]

Or as it has so often been said, if you have the Word and not the Spirit, you'll dry up. If you have the Spirit and not the Word you'll blow up. But if you have the Spirit and the Word together you'll grow up!

There are grave dangers in misunderstanding the Word of God through glibly accepting traditional interpretations. We need to make sure that Scripture determines our experience, and not let our experience, or lack of it, determine our Scripture. I accept the whole of the Scriptures as the revealed Word of God for all time, unless it is subsequently reversed in the Scripture. For example, 'You have heard that it was said, "An eye for an eye and a tooth for a tooth". But I say to you . . . ' (Matt. 5:38–9). The man who takes the Scriptures and says that verse was for 2,000 years ago, this one is for now, that one is for 2,000 years in the future, is as guilty of desecrating the Word of God as any liberal or modernist has ever been. Jesus said, 'Truly, truly, I say to you, he who believes in me will also do the works that I do; and greater works than these will he do' (John 14:12). Our God is not like a battery running down in power as the years go by. What he has done in the past he can still do today, and far greater things than Jesus did, *he has said* we are going to do!

The question might well be asked, in all seriousness, if we are under a different dispensation from the early church, why is it that almost every major revival has been accompanied by the same power signs and manifestations of the Spirit as those recorded in Acts? Could the answer be that rather than God decreeing a different dispensation the true fact of the matter is that Christians have lost that closeness of relationship which Jesus offers? When referring to the disappearance from the Church of the gifts of the Holy Spirit John Wesley commented: 'The causes of their decline was not, as has vulgarly been supposed, because there is no more need for them, because all the world were become Christians . . . the real cause was: the love of many, almost all so called Christians, was waxed cold . . . this was the real cause why the extraordinary gifts of the Holy Spirit were no longer to be found in the Christian church, because the Christians were turned heathen again, and had only a dead form left.'

Much of the controversy over the person and work of the Holy Spirit has been based on alarming misunderstandings. So much of the argument has been based on terminology surrounding what has been termed the 'charismatic movement', rather than concentrating on the issues involved. Those issues are:

1. We need to go further on in our personal relationship with the Lord so that we come actually to 'know' him and not be satisfied with just knowing about him. For so long we have been content with just taking Bible reading, church going, and praying into our old lifestyles. We have missed out on the glorious liberating truth that God actually wants us to come into deep, intimate, personal relationship with him.

Evangelism can never flourish until our churches, youth groups and evangelistic works are filled with men and women who are not satisfied with merely knowing about God but are pushing on to actually know him in the reality of personal experience.

It is so easy to see Christianity in terms of correct doctrine rather than in-depth experience, for doctrine is so less demanding. That is not to say that our doctrine should not be correct, rather it must never be a substitute for that knowledge of the holy one which is our birthright as children of the King. Paul pleaded 'that I may know him', and so should we. The sad truth for so many today is that 'To most people God is an inference, not a reality. He is a deduction from evidence which they consider adequate; but he remains personally unknown to the individual. For millions of Christians God is no more real than he is to the non-Christian.[6]

The re-emphasis on the need to really know God has come just in time. In practical terms three things have been underlined.

(a) The need to rediscover genuine Christian meditation. To take time, not just five minutes per day, with the Lord. To develope through prayer and study of the Word of God a deeper relationship with the almighty.
(b) The importance of communing with God in all that we say and do throughout the day. To begin to practise the presence of God.
(c) The tremendous potential of surrendering our bodies to be containers for the Spirit of God to indwell.

We were, in one way, made to be mugs! In other words we must be pots or containers for God to fill and through which he can express his love.

2. Rather than resting on a conversion experience we should look for a continuing, developing relationship with Jesus, a relationship which is deepening day by day.

The Scriptures clearly indicate that the Christian life is a spiritual life, and, as such, can only be lived in the power of the Holy Spirit and not in our own strength, that of the flesh. For so many of us our Christian lives fall flat after conversion, becoming just a really hard grind – living in the past with very little strength for the present. We become so unaware of that power, peace and vitality which accompany the presence of the Holy Spirit, that even our faces tend to betray our lack of joy. The Westminster Shorter Catechism states that 'the chief end of man is to glorify God, and to enjoy him for ever'. We cannot live on past experiences of God, however precious they may be. When we do our serenity too easily turns into a stony sobriety which may befit an Englishman but never a Christian!

We need to remember the word God gave to Isaiah – 'Remember not the former things, nor consider the things of old. Behold I am doing a new thing; now it springs forth, do you not perceive it?' (43:18–19). To have a pedigree is not necessarily a bad thing and to look back on the good things that God has done for us can be a very real encouragement but to attempt to live on the glories of the past and ignore the bitter realities of the present will always be fatal. The question must never be, 'What did God mean to us yesterday?' but 'What does God mean to us today?' That is why Paul writes 'Be filled with the Holy Spirit' (Eph. 5:18). The tense used in the original Greek is the aorist tense and does not refer to just a once and for all instance but an ongoing experience. A better translation from the Greek, although it would be very bad English, is 'Continue to being filled with the Holy Spirit.'

Dwight L. Moody was once addressing a nineteenth-century British congregation on this theme and many were offended. Afterwards one or two of the leaders and clergy took Moody to one side and asked, 'Why do you say that we need to go on being filled with the Holy Spirit – we've been filled, twenty years ago or thirty years ago, why do we need to go on being filled?' Moody's reply remains, to this day, an absolute classic – 'I need to be filled with the Spirit every moment of every day, because I leak!' I believe that today we are still a very leaky people and desperately need to know the power of God at work in our hearts and lives – not yesterday, but everyday!

3. The third crucial issue that the present 'charismatic movement', if it can be called that, has drawn our attention to is the whole concept of 'Baptism in the Holy Spirit'. This has really proved to be a desperately thorny issue. Allegations have been raised of dividing the body of Christ into 'haves' and 'have nots', of first-class and

second-class Christians, etc, etc. Some have even gone so far as to denounce the whole issue as being entirely 'of the Devil'!

This viewpoint can hardly be tenable, at least not from the standpoint that the whole Scriptures are the inspired word of God for now, and not just for yesterday. John the Baptist foretold that Jesus would baptise men and women with the Holy Spirit. All four gospels record that Jesus was baptised with the Holy Spirit. Jesus promised that same enduement of power to his disciples and made it the pre-requisite for their involvement in evangelism. It certainly does seem to have been the norm in the early church for the apostles were surprised to find Christians who had not received the baptism and immediately sent their two key men to ensure that the church did receive from the hand of God everything which he had for them.

A word of warning should perhaps be given to those individuals or churches who would oppose any such move of God among them, and it comes straight from the lips of Gamaliel: 'So in the present case, I tell you, keep away from these men, and let them alone. For if this plan or this undertaking is of men, it will fail; but if it is of God, you will not be able to overthrow them. You might even be found opposing God' (Acts 5:38–9).

A similar caution should be expressed to the other side of the issue. We are far too quick to write off those who do not have the same ideology or experience of God, as we have. God has always been the God of unity rather than of uniformity – he does not make everyone the same and does not necessarily deal with everybody in the same way. The question must never be, 'How are we being filled with the Holy Spirit?' it must be, 'Are we being filled with the Holy Spirit?' Whether God chooses to work by baptism in the Holy Spirit, release of the Spirit, filling with the Holy Spirit, or progressive sanctification is entirely up to him.

The blessing of a re-emphasis on the baptism of the Holy Spirit has been the attention it has drawn to the need in

138

some of a crisis experience in their spiritual lives. That must never replace an ongoing experience of the Spirit in our lives but it can be the start of one. In making that statement there is no inference that the Holy Spirit does not come to live within us at conversion, he obviously does – but the Old Testament talks much about the Holy Spirit coming upon people, and anointing them with power. Often that is what is needed today.

Each Christian receives the Holy Spirit from God at conversion, and the Spirit then comes to live within them. In John we read that Jesus breathed on his disciples and said 'receive the Holy Spirit' (20:22). When Jesus said something, it happened. Why then was Pentecost important?

For each one of us there is a big difference between allowing the Holy Spirit to live in us and letting him actually control our lives. To Jesus he came as a dove because there was no need for cleansing, but to the disciples the Spirit came with tongues of fire to burn out that which was of sin and self so that they could be filled with him. Then the power of God could be released within them and their lives could fully glorify Jesus. So many of us today are lacking that power and authority. If we know Christ's filling, directing and fulfilment and if there is no sense of dissatisfaction and disenchantment, then we do not need to look for more. But if not then perhaps the words of R. A. Torrey will be helpful.

Why shall we desire the baptism in the Spirit? In order that God may be glorified in our being baptised or filled with the Holy Spirit. Because we can no longer endure it, that God should be any longer dishonoured by the low level of our living, and by the ineffectiveness of our service; in order that God may be glorified by our being empowered to lead such lives as honour him . . . and when we get to praying for the baptism in the Spirit along that line, it will not be many hours before we are thus baptised with the Spirit of God.

We should never elevate any single experience of the love and power of God to a position where it condemns our brothers and sisters to believing that they are less spiritual than we are. Nor should we demand that everybody requires the same crisis experience as we have had. Instead, we should recognise that our living God treats us all as individuals. I get frustrated because he so often does not do what I would do! Instead he lovingly deals with us in his own way, but to one end, that we might reflect the love and glory of Jesus.

If we would stop allowing our personal insecurities to dictate to our minds the idea that God must never deal with any one else in a different way to that which he has used in our life, and would simply accept what our God is doing in one another, then our conversation about the Spirit of God would never cause division. The Holy Spirit will never divide those who truly love Jesus, that is something which only the mind of man can boast of doing!

4. At last, we are today hearing good news of new power and vitality in daily Christian living. No single experience of the activity of the Holy Spirit within the life of the believer can be an end in itself. Like conversion, we need to daily grow in all that God is doing within us. No single experience can be regarded as the antidote to all the problems of Christian life – in fact, a whole new set of problems may emerge. As an Anglican vicar said when describing the results within his congregation of their seeing a real move of the Spirit of God among them, 'We do not have less problems, but more; but we thank God, they are now the problems of life, whereas before they were the problems of death.'

There is no easy pathway to a simple Christian life. In fact things become much harder as we go on with the Lord because the Devil is allowed to test us more as our power to resist grows stronger. This release of the power and energy of the Holy Spirit which is so necessary comes only as God is allowed gently t. break us, emptying us of ourselves so that we may be filled in every area of our lives with his power and love.

I know a particular lady who is very tidy. All the rubbish that she finds lying around the house – scraps of paper, pins, shirt buttons, etc – she picks up, gathers together and puts straight into the vase on the mantelpiece. Suppose her husband comes in with a beautiful rose specially picked for his wife, and places it in the vase. Within six hours it is dead! If only he had emptied out the rubbish and filled the vase with fresh water – then the rose would have blossomed beautifully. If the love, power, energy and vitality of God is to blossom in us then we need to be emptied, and to be filled daily.

Andrew Murray put it like this: 'Lest any should have a wrong impression as to what it is to be filled with the Spirit, let me say that it does not mean a state of high excitement, or of absolute perfection, or a state in which there will be no growth. No. Being filled with his Spirit is simply this – having my whole nature yielded to his power. When the whole soul is yielded to the Holy Spirit, God himself will fill it.'

The surrender is leading to a new vitality and spontaneity in Christian living. No longer is the emphasis on bitter drudgery. As we learn that the message of Christianity is not a changed life but an exchanged life, so we are rediscovering the thrill of liberty as we allow the living Jesus to come and live his resurrection life in us. I am intimately involved – but no longer do I have to try to live the life of Christ for him, instead he comes to live it in me. By his Spirit.

Why then do we lack power? The answer for the twentieth-century British church lies here:

1. Because we are not prepared to believe God for what he has promised.

2. Because we are self-indulgent, uncharitable, censorious, self-dependent, revengeful and denominationally selfish.

3. Because we resist conviction of sin, making restitution to those we have injured or confessing our faults.

4. Because we are prejudiced, resentful, dogmatic, proud and full of wordly ambition.

5. Because we resist, grieve and quench the Holy Spirit.

6. Because we are bad-tempered, dishonest, lazy, impatient, negligent, we have our priorities wrong and lack total commitment and consecration.

Why do we lack power in our work and witness? Why is our evangelism devoid of the thrust and dynamism of the early church? Could it be because we lack that authority which the spirit of God always brings? Charles Finney commented that 'The disciples were Christians before the Day of Pentecost, and, as such, had a measure of the Holy Spirit. They must have had the peace of sins forgiven, and of a justified state, but yet they had not the enduement of power necessary to the accomplishment of the work assigned them. They had the peace which Christ had *given* them but not the *power* which he had promised.'[7]

If we need to reach our contemporaries with the same power possessed by the early church then we need to rediscover that same power and anointing with which they could reach their generation. Throughout the Christian centuries there have been times when the church and her members have made that discovery and turned their society upside down.

We will never achieve this out of our own human efforts. The only power that God recognises in his church is the power of his Spirit. There is nothing wrong with a trained and devoted intellect, except its utter uselessness apart from the anointing Spirit.

Watchman Nee used to recount the story of how he and a friend once saw a drowning man. Because Nee's friend was a far better swimmer than he was, he waited for his friend to rescue the drowning man. Meanwhile the man went under the water for the first time. Nee was taking his own jacket off while the man went under for the second time and his friend still did nothing. It was only when the man sank for the third and final time that Nee's friend dived in, swam underwater, retrieved the man, pulled him to the side so that Nee could haul him up to the bank. 'But why?' was Nee's question. He couldn't understand why his normally kind friend had allowed the man to suffer so much before rescuing him. The reason? 'I had to wait until he'd given up hope and stopped struggling.'

In exactly the same way God waits for us to learn that lesson. To learn that apart from his Spirit we can achieve nothing. 'For I know that nothing good dwells within me, that is, in my flesh. I can will what is right, but I cannot do it' (Rom. 7:18). So what is the alternative, if any? Do we continue in sins in order that grace may be multiplied – J. B. Phillips version of Paul's reply must be an Englishman's classic, 'What a ghastly thought!' I can no longer be condemned because 'the law of the Spirit of life in Christ Jesus has set me free from the law of sin and death' (Rom. 8:2).

We must recognise our need to live each day filled with the Holy Spirit. For too long we have run in panic from the simple, basic life-transforming things which God wants to do within each one of us. J. I. Brice has so aptly put it, 'The church has halted somewhere between Calvary and Pentecost.' Rufus Mosely has commented, 'The average spiritual temperature in the church is so low that when a healthy man comes along everyone thinks he has a fever,' and Leonard Ravenhill summarises the argument, 'Warned of false fire by fireless men we so often settle for no fire at all.'

It is time for the church of Christ and those of us who are part of it, to seek again the reality that alone comes from the Spirit of God. If we are to challenge our society with the good news of the Christ who she so actively rejects then we must find a new power from outside ourselves. That power rests within God himself. To some of us the call will come simply to humble ourselves and pray; others will need to seek ministry and help. The end result must be the same – lives filled and renewed with the Spirit of God, then, and only then, will the world see and recognise the life of Jesus reflected in us.

A few years ago while conducting a mission in a southern coastal town I met a roly-poly, cheerful individual named Charlie. He was a university post-graduate student and a pillar of the local church, twenty-two years old and a mature Christian. One night Charlie came to me with tears in his eyes: 'Clive,' he asked, 'I want a straight answer to a straight question.'

'Okay. Fire ahead,' I replied.

'Why, when non-Christians took note that the early church had been with Jesus, do none of my friends see Jesus in me?'

That is a question which one can never really answer, so we simply got on our knees together and prayed quietly for Jesus to take Charlie's life in its every part and fill him continually with his Holy Spirit. Afterwards I heard this story: two days later when Charlie was working in a laboratory with a Pakistani friend he was asked, 'Charlie, what happened to you forty-eight hours ago. You're a different kind of Charlie!'

He still is a different kind of Charlie today, but a number of non-Christians have met Jesus because they first saw him living in Charlie. Is that what others see in you, or is there so much of you that Jesus is obliterated? On your knees in simple submission is where we can encounter Jesus in new and deeper ways. When we die to ourselves and allow Christ alone to live with us – then we will transform our society. Revival will always begin, not in the world, but among the people of God, so that as our light shines in the darkness people will be attracted to Jesus, and evangelism will flow out of the witness of God's people.

Then we can proclaim with all the children of the King, 'I have been crucified with Christ; and it is no longer I who live, but Christ who lives in me' (Gal. 2:20).

Notes

Chapter 1

1. Samuel Escobar, *Social Concern and World Evangelism* (Herald Press, USA).
2. Paul Tournier, *A Place For You* (SCM Press, 1968).
3. Malcolm Muggeridge, *Another King* (St Andrew Press, 1968).
4. John Stott *et al*, International Congress on World Evangelisation – Lausanne 1974.
5. A. W. Tozer, *The Root of the Righteous* (Christian Publications, USA).
6. Alan Richardson, *A Theological Word Book of the Bible* (SCM Press, 1963).
7. David Watson, *I Believe in Evangelism* (Hodder & Stoughton, 1976).
8. A. W. Tozer, 'The Old Cross and the New' (published in *The Best of A. W. Tozer*, Bake Books, USA).

Chapter 2

1. Paul E. Billheimer, *Don't waste your Sorrows* (Christian Literature Crusade, USA).
2. Lesslie Newbigin, *The Household of God* (SCM Press).
3. Gerald Coates, *That You May Not Sin* (Facet Publications).
4. Howard Snyder, *New Wineskins* (Marshall, Morgan & Scott, 1977).
5. J. B. Phillips, Introduction to Acts.

Chapter 3

1. David Watson, *I Believe in the Church* (Hodder & Stoughton, 1978).
2. Juan Carlos Ortiz, *Cry of the Human Heart* (Lakeland, 1977).
3. A. W. Tozer.

Chapter 4

1. Winston S. Churchill, House of Commons 13th May, 1939.
2. A. W. Tozer, *Paths to Power* (Lakeland, 1964).
3. T. Rice and A. Lloyd Webber, *Joseph and his Amazing Technicolour Dreamcoat*.
4. Quoted in David Watson, *I Believe in the Church*.
5. Watchman Nee, *The Spiritual Man*, Vol 1 (Christian Fellowship Publishers Inc., USA).
6. C. S. Lewis, *Screwtape Letters* (Fontana, 1955).
7. *Macbeth*, Act IV scene 3.
8. C. S. Lewis, *Screwtape Letters*, Preface.

Chapter 5

1. *Paix et Liberte*,
2. Harvey Cox, *The Secular City* (Penguin, 1968).
3. Leonard Ravenhill, *Why Revival Tarries* (Bethany Fellowship, USA).
4. Max Warren, *I Believe in the Great Commission* (Hodder & Stoughton, 1976).
5. Howard Snyder, 'The Church as God's Agent in Evangelism' (published in *Let the whole earth hear his voice*).
6. A. W. Tozer, *Paths to Power*.
7. Tom Walker, *Open to God* (Grove Books, 1977).
8. Donald McGavren, *Understanding Church Growth* (Eerdman's, USA).
9. Lawrence O. Richards, *A New Face for the Church* (Zondervan, USA).

Chapter 6

1. *My Fair Lady*
2. Michael Ramsey, Foreword to *Gathered into One*, William R. Davies (Faith Press, 1975).
3. A. W. Tozer, *Of God and Men* (Christian Publications, USA).
4. Francis Schaeffer, 'Form and Freedom in the Church (published in *Let the whole earth hear his voice*).

Chapter 7

1. David Watson, *I Believe in Evangelism*.
2. D. M. Panton, quoted in *Rain from Heaven* by Arthur Wallis (Hodder and Stoughton, 1979).
3. A. W. Tozer, *Of God and Men*.
4. A. W. Tozer, 'How to be Filled with the Holy Spirit' (published in *The Best of A. W. Tozer*).
5. Hans Kung, *The Church* (Search Press, 1969).
6. A. W. Tozer, *The Pursuit of God* (Lakeland, 1969).
7. Charles Finney, *Power from on High* (Victory Press, 1944).

Additional reading list

Chapter 1   David Watson, *I Believe in Evangelism*
             Leighton Ford, *The Christian Persuader*
             A. W. Tozer, *The Divine Conquest*

Chapter 2   Luis Palau, *The Moment to Shout*
             Juan Carlos Ortiz, *The Cry of the Human Heart*
             Alan Redpath, *Victorious Christian Service*

Chapter 3   Howard Snyder, *New Wineskins*
             David Watson, *I Believe in the Church*
             Leonard Ravenhill, *Why Revival Tarries*
             John Balchin, *What the Bible says about the Church*

Chapter 4   J. Wesley White, *The Devil*
             David Watson, *God's Freedom Fighters*
             John White, *The Fight*

Chapter 5   Donald McGavran, *Understanding Church Growth*
             BMMF, *Can British Churches Grow?*
             Virgil Gerber, *God's Way to keep a Church Going and Growing*

Chapter 6   Francis Schaeffer, *The Church before the Watching World*
             William Davies, *Gathered into One*
             Michael Griffiths, *Cinderella with Amnesia*

Chapter 7   Michael Green, *I Believe in the Holy Spirit*
            Michael Harper, *Power for the Body of Christ*
            Eric Delve, *To Boldly Go*

Epilogue
So don't just sit there . . .

This book is not intended merely as an academic treatise adding to your store of information or good teaching. It is written as a spur to action. Unfortunately, even faced with a direct challenge to repentance and bold action, most of us still slip all too easily into a mood where we indulge vague feelings of desire for change and even vaguer good intentions. This is not the way to see the radical transformation of the church in our country that we all long to see.

Most of you will know that Clive Calver is the National Director of British Youth for Christ and it is my privilege to work alongside him as National Evangelist. When we consider what God has done in Youth for Christ in the last few years we are utterly amazed. We are convinced also that all that has happened so far has been only preparation for the real thing. We believe that the Almighty Father is about to pour out his Spirit on Britain as never before and the only condition is that his people should be totally available to him.

Will you consider whether the Lord wants you to share in the work of Youth for Christ?

Each year, in association with *Buzz* magazine, we hold an exciting and challenging Christian holiday called Spring Harvest.

There are local branches of Youth for Christ all over the country and new ones are opening all the time – we can tell you the location of your nearest branch.

Many of these branches employ a schools worker who spends the majority of his time aiding the teaching programme in local schools doing absolutely vital gospel groundwork.

Then, in co-operation with a leading publisher, we are offering for hire specially selected films, relevant to the harsh world of today.

All over the country there are evangelists and musicians in fellowship with Youth for Christ. They use all kinds of methods and operate in many different styles. One of them could suit your event.

We exist as a missionary agency to serve the local church and would love to help you in any way we can.

As you can imagine, a work as big as this needs much support; first in prayer, second in work, third in finance.

If you want to help or need information about any of the above aspects of the work of BYFC please write to:

> John Earwicker,
> Asst. National Director,
> BYFC,
> 52/54 Lichfield Street,
> Wolverhampton,
> WV1 1DG

I would like to add a personal invitation. If you would like to explore the possibility of holding an evangelistic mission/crusade/festival in your town and would like to draw on our experience, do feel free to contact me at the above address.

May the Lord be with you as you consider action for him and his gospel.

Don't just sit there . . . do something.

> Yours in Christ
> ERIC DELVE
> National Evangelist
> British Youth for Christ